Psychological Types

Psychology at Work
Series editor: Clive Fletcher

This series interprets and examines people's work behaviour from the perspective of occupational psychology. Each title focuses on a central issue in management, emphasizing the role of the individual's workplace experience.

Books in the series include:

Creating the Healthy Organization
Well-being, Diversity and Ethics at Work
Sue Newell

Impression Management
Building and Enhancing Reputations at Work
Paul Rosenfeld, Robert A. Giacalone
and Catherine A. Riordan

Managing Employee Performance
Design and Implementation in Organizations
Richard S. Williams

Managing Innovation and Change
A Critical Guide for Organizations
Nigel King and Neil Anderson

Managing Teams
A Strategy for Success
Nicky Hayes

Psychological Types at Work
An MBTI® Perspective
Rowan Bayne

Recruitment and Selection
A Framework for Success
Dominic Cooper, Ivan T. Robertson and Gordon Tinline

Psychology
at Work

Psychological Types at Work

An MBTI® Perspective

Rowan Bayne

THOMSON

™

Australia • Canada • Mexico • Singapore • Spain • United Kingdom • United States

Psychological Types at Work: An MBTI® Perspective

Copyright © Rowan Bayne 2004

The Thomson logo is a registered trademark used herein under licence.

For more information, contact Thomson Learning, High Holborn House, 50–51 Bedford Row, London WC1R 4LR or visit us on the World Wide Web at: http://www.thomsonlearning.co.uk

British Library Cataloguing-in-Publication Data
A catalogue record for this book is available from the British Library

ISBN 1-86152-990-2

First edition published by Thomson Learning 2004

Typeset by LaserScript, Mitcham, Surrey
Printed in Great Britain by TJ International, Padstow, Cornwall

Contents

Figures

Tables

Boxes

Series editor's preface

Understanding the psychology of individuals and teams is of prime importance in work settings as rapid and far-reaching changes continue to occur. Organizational structures are shifting radically to the point where individual managers and professionals have far greater autonomy, responsibility and accountability. Organizations are seeking to reduce central control and to 'empower' individual employees. These employees combine in teams that are frequently cross-functional and project based rather than hierarchical in their construction. The traditional notion of careers has changed; increasingly, an individual's career is less likely to be within a single organization, which has implications for how organizations command loyalty and commitment. The full impact of information technology has now been felt, with all the consequences this has for the nature of work and the reactions of those doing it.

The capacity of people to cope with the scale and speed of change has become a major issue and the literature on work stress only increases. The belief in the importance of individuals' cognitive abilities and personality make-up in determining what they achieve and how they contribute to teamwork has been demonstrated in the explosive growth in organizations' use of psychometric tests and related procedures. Perhaps more than ever before, analysing and understanding the experience of work from a psychological perspective is necessary to achieve the twin goals of effective performance and quality of life. Unfortunately, it is the latter of these that all too often seems to be overlooked in the concern to create competitive, performance-driven or customer-focused cultures within companies.

It is no coincidence that the rise in the study of business ethics and increasing concern over issues of fairness paralleled many of the organizational changes of the late twentieth century. Ultimately, an imbalance between the aims and needs of the employees and the aims and needs of the organization is self-defeating. One of the widely recognized needs for the twenty-first century is for a greater emphasis on innovation rather than on simply reacting to pressures. However, psychological research and theory indicate that innovation is much more likely to take place where individuals feel secure enough to take the risks involved, and where organizational reward systems encourage experimentation and exploration – which they have signally failed to do in the last century. Seeking to help organizations realize the potential of their workforce in a mutually enhancing way is the business challenge psychology has to meet.

The central theme of the *Psychology at Work* series is to interpret and explain people's work behaviour in the context of a continually evolving pattern of change, and to do so from the perspective of occupational and organizational psychology. Each of the books draws together academic research and practitioner experience, relying on empirical studies, practical examples and case studies to communicate their ideas. The reader, whether a student, manager or psychologist, will find that they provide a succinct summary of accumulated knowledge and a guide to how to apply it in business. The themes of some of the books cover traditional areas of occupational psychology, while others focus on topics that cut across such boundaries, tackling subjects that are of growing interest and prominence. They are directly relevant for practitioners, consultants and students of HR and occupational psychology but much of what they deal with is of great value to managers, and students of management, more generally. This broad appeal is demonstrated by the fact that an earlier version of the series, the *Essential Business Psychology* series, was highly commended by the Management Consultancies Association book award. The *Psychology at Work* series shares the aims, and some of the titles, as the original series but the individual books have been substantially updated and the range of titles is expanded. Although the books share a common aim and series heading, they have not been forced into a rigid stylistic format. In keeping with the times, the authors have had a good deal of autonomy in deciding how to organize and present their work. I think all of them have done an excellent job; I hope you will find that too.

Clive Fletcher

Acknowledgements

My very warm thanks to Rae Carlson and Nissim Levy for publishing an article in the 1973 *Journal of Personality* called 'Studies of Jungian typology: memory, social perception and social action'. I came across their article in about 1979 and was very struck by its clarity, by the fact that I could easily understand the statistics and, most of all, by the potential of the personality theory they had investigated and the strength and practical relevance of their findings. The theory was Isabel Myers's clarification and development of some of Jung's ideas and I've been intrigued by it ever since.

To the thousands of people whose possible types I've observed, thought about and talked about since that moment in a library in 1979.

To Tracy Boakes for wordprocessing my many messy drafts, positively, resiliently and with great speed.

To Sally Close for skilful copy-editing.

To Susanne Masters for two extracts from her MBTI essay (in Chapter 2).

To OKA for permission to reproduce the modified stick figures (Chapter 2).

To CPP for special permission to quote modified versions of Tables of UK and US MBTI types (also in Chapter 2).

To OPP for permission to reproduce 'MBTI holidays' (Chapter 3).

MBTI®, *Myers-Briggs*® and *Myers-Briggs Type Indicator*® are trademarks or registered trademarks of the Myers-Briggs Type Indicator Trust in the United States and other countries.

Introduction and overview

This book applies the theory underlying the Myers-Brigg Type Indicator (MBTI) questionnaire and the related research to various aspects of work. MBTI theory is Isabel Myers's clarification and development of the least abstruse (her term) of Jung's ideas about personality. Its most distinctive features are that it takes individuality unusually seriously and its positive and constructive tone. I take the most relevant ideas and evidence, integrate them, critique them, compare them with mainstream occupational psychology where it seems useful, and discuss their implications for managers, HR professionals and consultants, and students on management and occupational psychology courses.

Overview

In Chapter 1, I first discuss the considerable success of MBTI theory and its strengths and limitations. The second part of the chapter focuses on effective use of the theory, including the role of evidence-based practice and four levels of application. The chapter ends with replies to questions about applying the theory which are frequently asked in MBTI workshops.

It's not legal or ethical to include the MBTI questionnaire itself in this book. Another questionnaire measure of the psychological types would also be unethical because it wouldn't have been validated and questionnaire results, especially expressed numerically, can too easily have a spurious authority. Therefore, in Chapter 2 I've introduced the theory in a way that tries to allow reasonably accurate assessment of all or part of your own type if you wish.

Alternatively, if you've already completed the MBTI questionnaire or another measure of the sixteen psychological types proposed by Myers, Chapter 2 can be a check on the accuracy of your results, a reminder of the theory, or an introduction to some new aspects of it. A further option built into the chapter is for you to apply MBTI theory to someone else, but not yourself. Chapter 2 reviews the central concept of preference, the four pairs of preferences, the four temperaments in Keirsey's model, type dynamics and type development. Like Chapter 1, it concludes with replies to frequently asked questions.

The applications at work chapters all discuss an MBTI perspective on aspects of what is variously called HRM, Occupational Psychology (in the UK), Work and Organizational Psychology (rest of Europe), Individual and Organizational Psychology (US), etc. The aspects are: careers (Chapter 3); selection (Chapter 4); time (Chapter 5); communication (Chapter 6); health (Chapter 7); coaching and counselling (Chapter 8); and leading and managing (Chapter 9).

1 Applying MBTI theory

In this chapter I first discuss MBTI theory's considerable success, its strengths and its limitations. Then I focus on two aspects of applying the theory: evidence-based practice and levels of application. In the final section, I give brief replies to questions on related topics which are often asked in courses and workshops.

MBTI theory is successful commercially and in terms of numbers of research papers and translations. The theory is generally applied through the MBTI questionnaire, which is the most widely used non-clinical measure of personality. The 2003 OPP catalogue calls it 'the most popular personality measure in the world' (p. 66) and it is reported as selling from two to three million copies per year, and has done so for many years (Myers *et al.*, 1998; CPP Catalog, 2001).

There is also a large and rapidly growing literature, both of empirical studies and applications. The Center for Applications of Psychological Type (CAPT) has an online bibliography which in 2002 contained nearly 8000 items (Styron, 2002), including 1542 doctorial dissertations. The *Journal of Psychological Type* has just reached its twenty-fifth anniversary (Carskadon, 2002), and in 1994 became part of the PsycINFO system of the American Psychological Association. This was an important recognition by mainstream psychology.

A further indication of success is the number of languages the MBTI questionnaire has been translated into. Commercial translations available in 2003 are listed in Table 1.1; translations restricted to researchers in Table 1.2; and translations in progress in Table 1.3.

Table 1.1	**Commercial translations**
	European English
	Australian English
	Bahasa Malay
	Chinese
	Dutch
	French (European)
	French (Canadian)
	German
	Italian
	Japanese
	Korean
	Norwegian
	Portuguese
	Spanish (United States, European, and Argentina)
	Swedish

Source: CAPT 2/03

Table 1.2	**Research translations**
	Afrikaans
	Arabic
	Czech
	Finnish
	Flemish
	Greek
	Hungarian
	Icelandic
	Slovak
	Thai
	Vietnamese
	Zulu

Source: CAPT 2/03

Strengths of MBTI theory and applications

I think there are five reasons or strengths which explain this sustained success: the positive tone of its descriptions of the personality types; the general nature of its aims and therefore the wide range of its applications; its versatility; the evidence for its validity; and, perhaps most arguably, the term 'type'. The first strength can also be seen as a

Table 1.3	**Translations in process**
	Albanian
	Bosnian
	Bulgarian
	Croatian
	Hungarian
	Latvian
	Macedonian
	Polish
	Serbian
	Slovenian
	Turkish

Source: CAPT 2/03

limitation, and I think the validity evidence is relatively good but with lots of scope for improvement.

Positive tone

The positive tone of the type descriptions is illustrated throughout Chapter 2 and discussed briefly there in comparison to five factor theory. The basic descriptions of the preferences, temperaments and types are glowing. They can seem relentlessly so – too good to be true. However, they do have a 'twist': that strengths have corresponding weaknesses. Thus, where one psychological type tends to be at its best, the opposite type tends to be weakest, and vice versa.

Aims

The theory's general aims are: (1) to help us understand and respect ourselves; and (2) to help us understand and respect others. There is a major emphasis on the 'constructive use of differences', as opposed to the decidedly unconstructive, but human tendency to judge people different to ourselves as stupid, inefficient, awkward or mad. More specific applications thus include team-building, relationship counselling and diversity awareness training as well as self-development, career development, leadership training, etc.

'Use of differences' may sound impersonal (like Human Resource Management) but the theory's tone is warm and positive and apart from its helping people to make sense of and value aspects of themselves that they've found difficult to express and aspects of other people that they've disparaged, it is this tone which explains its success. It also makes the abstract ideal of respecting differences in personality much more concrete.

Versatility

The theory's versatility is evident in its wide range of applications, and also in the various levels of these (Bayne, 2004). At the simplest level, one of the pairs of preferences can provide a useful insight; at the most complex level, there is type dynamics, including the so-called 'Shadow' side of personality. Between the preferences and type dynamics are four temperaments, sixteen types and other combinations of preferences, with type development a constant extra factor.

Evidence for validity

The evidence for the validity of MBTI theory is substantial, though much more so at the level of the preferences than that of type dynamics (Bayne, 1995, 2004; Myers *et al.*, 1998). The two main sources are findings on the Big Five theory of personality, which has dominated mainstream personality research for several years, much as MBTI theory has dominated applied personality theory, and findings from studies of the theory itself, most of it using the MBTI questionnaire.

Big Five theory has been investigated very extensively and rigorously, and four of its five factors are strongly related to the four preferences in MBTI theory (e.g. McCrae and Costa, 1989; Furnham, 1996). The validity of MBTI theory, at the level of the preferences, is therefore supported by research on the Big Five. I think the relationship between measures of the two sets of characteristics is ideal for MBTI theory: strong enough to be good evidence for its validity, but leaving room for different interpretations of the meaning of each preference or factor.

This convergence between the two theories is also encouraging for personality theory generally: two questionnaires developed in radically different traditions agree closely on four major characteristics of personality. Indeed, McCrae and Costa, though generally critical of MBTI theory, comment that the MBTI descriptions are 'reasonably good' (p. 35). The two theories differ in 'tone' (illustrated in Chapter 2), their attitude towards the term 'type' (next section), and of course the fifth factor, Anxiety (discussed in the section on limitations of MBTI theory in this chapter).

The MBTI questionnaire itself has also been quite widely researched. Some of the research is discussed in this book, for example the relationships between psychological type and choice of career (Chapters 3 and 8). Other research is reviewed in Hammer (1996), Myers *et al.* (1998) and Bayne (1995, 2004). The validity evidence so far is less strong for type dynamics than for the preferences. However, there does seem to be more to each type than just adding the four preferences together. In any case, most of the applications discussed in this book are at the level of the preferences.

Type

'Type' is a dangerous word for MBTI theory because it can be interpreted as a rigid and suffocating box, in a 'this is the way you are so get used to it' way. It may also have connotations of mysticism and charlatanism. However, I think the strengths of the term outweigh its problems. First, type in MBTI theory has a more flexible meaning than such fears and rejections allow. It says that each person is an individual, that their type is an important element in that individuality, and that our behaviour is influenced by our type, but certainly not restricted to it. Further, in its MBTI theory meaning, it implies that people are very similar in some respects (nearly everyone uses all the preferences some of the time) but also profoundly and fundamentally different (people are different in kind, not just in degree). I think this latter meaning is its main strength: 'type' emphasizes the fundamental nature of differences more than say 'style' and – unfortunately – 'preference'.

The degree of consistency in people's behaviour is part of the issue here. One view is that people are dynamic, changeable, complicated. 'I vary' could be the rallying cry. 'I contain multitudes'. And so we do, but for personality to be a meaningful idea, we also need some consistency. We're not robots and we're not totally variable either.

I think the term 'type' as used in MBTI theory (and 'preference', discussed in Chapter 2) reflect this reality well.

A second strength of 'type' is that it implies personality structure and organization. Trait theories currently dominate the personality literature, and they are analogous to describing an animal, say, in terms of speed of movement, size and furriness. This animal is quick, medium size and furry (traits) or a leopard (type). The trait labels communicate valuable information but not as much as the type label, or as economically (Bayne, 2004).

Of course, the leopard analogy isn't a direct parallel with people. It's less easy to make an accurate judgement of a person's type than an animal's, because we are skilful at faking behaviour as well as genuinely versatile, and because our backgrounds (family, culture, etc.) are much more complex. Development is much more straightforward in leopards than in people, and so are motives.

A third strength of type is related to the leopard analogy. It is that many people – proportion unknown – use their own type theories to guide their behaviour. These personal theories tend to use prototypes or fuzzy types, i.e. categories which, like MBTI types, fit some people more closely than others. For example, a robin is a prototypical bird, and an ostrich less so. The fact that many people develop their own type theories is a further strength of MBTI theory; it makes it more attractive and easy to use. On the other hand, most of these 'lay' type theories could be improved by better categories and more cautious use of them.

Limitations of MBTI theory and applications

I think MBTI theory and application have three main limitations: the major personality trait of Anxiety (or Neuroticism) is missing; there is no rigorous measure of type development; and it is sometimes misused. The first two limitations can also be seen as strengths in part and misuses are probably inevitable but can be reduced.

Anxiety

As touched on earlier, the four MBTI preferences correlate quite well with four of the Big Five factors. The other factor is Anxiety, which is definitely a major individual difference. It would be possible to treat it as a preference and therefore to interpret it positively, to maintain the positive tone of MBTI descriptions, but this would stretch its meaning too far. Characteristics like chronic worrying, dejection, tension, moodiness and low energy, even though they may be associated with sensitivity (in a positive sense) and emotional richness, are not an asset at work or generally. What people who are high in trait Anxiety can do is develop effective coping strategies and adjust their lives accordingly. They can also take pleasure in not being emotionally bland. However, to include Anxiety in the MBTI questionnaire or in descriptions of the psychological types would detract too much from its aims. Indeed, the descriptions seem to me to assume low anxiety.

A similar limitation of the MBTI questionnaire is that it doesn't include a measure of 'intelligence'. Again, there is a benefit as well as a loss. The benefit is that the theory offers a broad conception of intelligence – indeed, four kinds, discussed in Chapter 10, or sixteen kinds (Lawrence, 1993). The limitation is that intelligence, in its mainstream psychology sense of 'g', is an influential individual difference.

Type development

Type development is central to applications of type (though often implicit) but it too is not measured by the MBTI questionnaire or, so far, by any rigorous method (Bayne, 2004). Rather, the descriptions of the types which are routinely used assume that reasonable type development is the norm. Although there is (from observation) considerable variation in type development, it seems to me from the validity evidence that reasonable type development actually is the norm.

Moreover, using a measure of type development – probably a battery of ability tests – would make applications of MBTI theory much more threatening. People would be likely to feel that their competencies were being assessed, and they'd be right. The notion of preference is a major strength in this way; it's very helpful that the MBTI questionnaire doesn't measure development, maturity or competence.

Misuses

A final limitation, of a different kind, is that the theory is sometimes misused. One misuse is to attempt to explain everything with it, but probably the major problem is that labels can be used to stereotype. An extreme example, at least if taken at face value, is a group of executives who were told by their managing director that they all had six months to become one of the types – their company's 'designated management type'. At a stroke, this grotesque policy not only shows a misunderstanding of what MBTI theory assumes about change, but also illustrates how *not* to value difference.

There are more subtle examples of misuse of the theory in the section on ethical application in Chapter 2. However, the dangers of misuse need to be balanced against the potential of *good* labels, used *well*, to clarify and liberate.

A different kind of misuse is that most text books in introductory psychology, personality theory and occupational psychology either ignore MBTI theory (bizarrely in view of its wide use) or treat it superficially, inaccurately, or both. Quite often, for example, in recent texts, the 1962 Manual is referred to rather than 1998 third edition or even the 1985 second edition. On the other hand, there are a few positive (and accurate!) citings, and the main strategy to bring about improved treatment is obvious: to add to the few MBTI studies that have been published in leading journals.

Evidence-based practice and MBTI theory

Evidence-based practice (EBP) has had a spectacular rise and expansion in a variety of disciplines, including HRM (Briner, 2000; Trinder with Reynolds, 2000). Sackett *et al.*'s 1997 book, *Evidence-Based Medicine*, has been particularly influential, and they defined evidence-based medicine as 'the conscientious, explicit and judicious use of current best evidence in making decisions about individual patients' (p.2). They also emphasized the roles of clinical expertise and patient choice. Substitute client, employees, organization, etc. for 'patient', and, at first sight – in HRM as in medicine – EBP seems obviously to be a good idea. *Of course* practitioners should take into account the most up-to-date and valid research findings rather than relying on their primary training, expert opinions, fashion and their own, necessarily limited, experience, and taking unjustified risks with ineffective or even harmful techniques and approaches.

However, applying EPB to work is problematic at each of three main stages: producing the evidence, making it accessible to practitioners, and implementing it. First, where many HRM techniques are concerned there isn't much good evidence as yet (Briner, 2000) and, on some questions, it may never exist. The complexities and cost of the research are just too great. This is true to a lesser extent in medicine, though there is still a lot we don't know about how the body works and about which treatments are most effective, despite the 'gold standard' method of randomized controlled trials (RCTs) being more feasible in medicine than in psychology. EBP is at an early stage of development even in medicine (Trinder with Reynolds, 2000).

Second, even the most rigorous research methods have significant limitations. For example, RCTs have proved dramatically valuable in medicine, with several treatments, at one time standard, shown to kill more patients than they cure (Wessely, 2001). However, RCTs look for overall effects – which intervention or technique is the most effective – when, as MBTI theory predicts, average differences sometimes conceal *opposing* effects, so that a particular intervention which is generally effective is actually counter-productive for some people. A related problem (though not one peculiar to RCTs) is that in order to interpret their results more straightforwardly, researchers deliberately exclude some participants, e.g. by gender or age, so the research participants may differ from the practitioner's clients or patients.

There are also problems with making the evidence available. Because there are sometimes hundreds of potentially relevant studies on one technique or question, keeping up with the literature in a broad discipline like HRM is impossible for a single person. The information overload is too great. In addition, judging the quality and relevance of findings when many studies are methodologically weak or flawed, while others are rigorous but irrelevant, is a highly skilled activity.

Finally, there are problems with implementing EBP. For example, presenting the best evidence to a client is not just a matter of providing information. (MBTI theory could be particularly useful here, for example Chapter 6 on communication and the section in Chapter 9 on problem management.) The problems with actually using the good evidence we have is highlighted by the argument that in some areas – selection and stress are the most obvious possibilities – we should stop gathering evidence and put our efforts into implementing what is already known. However, it's not going to happen. Moreover, even in an area like selection, there are many unanswered and potentially fruitful questions (Robertson and Smith, 2001).

A political problem is that EBP could be used to *exclude* certain techniques and strategies. This is a method of rationing in the name of efficiency, but one that could mean the loss of effective but difficult to evaluate strategies. More subtly, it could mean that strategies which are more effective over the medium- or long-term are used less than those which have a quick impact and then fade.

There are counter-arguments for each of these problems. For example, in medicine, literature reviews are carried out by experts and made widely available. Thus someone else does the 'keeping up', or at least the most difficult and time-consuming part. However, for the purposes of this book, the problems with applying EBP to work have two implications. First, I see the professional autonomy of practitioners as central. Second, at the same time practice needs to be informed and guided by evidence as much as possible, for both ethical and legal reasons – i.e. practitioners generally want their work to be as effective as it can be but also need, increasingly, to be able to defend their decisions, sometimes in court.

Clarity about the *process* of integrating experience and evidence is likely to be useful in both respects, and Anderson *et al.* (2001) provide a framework. They used the dimensions of relevance and rigour to suggest four approaches to science, which they called Popularist, Pedantic, Puerile and Pragmatic. Popularist Science is high on practical relevance but low on rigour. They remark that 'In the USA, research of this sort has been termed "junk science", and has been viewed as inadmissible evidence in a court of law' (p. 393). Pedantic Science is high on rigour but low on relevance, while Puerile Science is neither rigorous nor relevant. In contrast, Pragmatic Science is both relevant and rigorous. It is also of course the approach which is consistent with EBP, and the one I try to take in this book, within the important limitations discussed above. In particular, the notion of 'evidence' needs to be a broad one (Anderson *et al.*, 2001; Robson, 2002).

Four levels of applying MBTI theory

1 General

At this level the theory is used to question and perhaps broaden assumptions about what people should be like, what is healthy and what is odd. It says that there are several radically different ways of being a happy and effective person. The theory can also be used to improve communications with groups of people by offering a wider range of information and choices to them, especially choices different to your own. You don't need to know the other person's or the particular group's temperaments or types for this general use, but knowledge of your own type should increase awareness of your most likely biases in this respect.

2 Communication style

Here the theory is used to match or challenge another person's 'language' or communication style at the time. This is said to be easier to observe than type (Chapter 6).

3 Preferences, types and temperaments

At this level, you observe the other person's preferences more or less formally. More sophisticated applications of MBTI theory are then possible, for example careers advice related to type. Explaining people to each other is also possible, using the ideas but not necessarily the terms: 'Some people ... but others ...'

4 Type dynamics and type development

This is the most sophisticated level of application, taking type dynamics and type development into account to ask such questions as:

- Is the person's dominant function the one they trust and use the most?
- Does their auxiliary function provide balance?

Each of the four levels includes the level or levels preceding it. This book is mainly concerned with level 3 applications, venturing occasionally into aspects of level 4, but only touches on the 'deepest' and most speculative levels of the theory.

Some questions and replies

The five questions discussed in this section are asked quite frequently in MBTI workshops and courses. Questions about the theory itself are discussed at the end of Chapter 2, because I'm trying to allow you the choice of coming fresh to the verifying your own type option which is the main theme of that chapter.

1 What about Jung?

There is disagreement about how closely related MBTI theory and Jungian theory are (Bayne, 1995). Isabel Myers saw her theory as applying Jung's but I think she undervalued her own contribution in selecting some of Jung's ideas, clarifying them and developing them. She wasn't just a translator.

Myers described Jung's *Psychological Types* as more 'abstruse' than her own work (Myers with Myers, 1980, p. 17). This is as a gentle criticism, and perhaps a compliment, because 'abstruse' means profound as well as obscure. Jung's writing can be contradictory and badly organized, but with occasional gems – and perhaps his contradictions just reflect an extraordinarily agile and rich mind. Jung's writing on type may be viewed as mainly of historical interest, but clearly his contribution deserves to be recognized.

2 How does MBTI theory relate to other personality theories?

There are different emphases (or more than that) within the MBTI approach, broadly a more psychodynamic approach (e.g. Quenk, 1993) and a more humanistic one (e.g. Kroeger and Thuesen, 1988). Essentially though, I see it as a fulfilment or self theory, in the same 'family' as Rogers, Maslow and Jourard (Bayne, 1995). Big Five or five factor theory, though most explicitly a trait theory, also has elements of this approach. Conversely, at the level of the preferences, MBTI theory is sometimes treated (or rather mistreated) as a trait theory.

MBTI theory also transcends the usual categories of personality theory. A recent, well-received framework illustrates this. Dan McAdams (1995) suggested that personality can be described at three levels:

1 Traits
2 Personal concerns
3 Integrative life stories

'Knowing a person well' therefore means knowing them at all these levels. McAdams' view is that level 1 is 'well-mapped' but that level 2, which includes motives, 'life tasks', etc. and level 3 are not, and that there may even be a level 4. MBTI theory includes elements of levels 1, 2 and 3 of McAdams's model of personality with life themes (Nardi, 1999) a possibility for 3, and thus offers quite a grand theory (Bayne, 2004), though McAdams would probably see this as premature.

3 What other measures of the types are there?

There are several other self-report questionnaires but none with anything like the validity evidence, or the wide use, of the MBTI questionnaire. Keirsey's Temperament Sorter II (in Keirsey 1998) has reliabilities which are adequate for research but a little low for use with individuals (Dodd and Bayne, submitted).

Most books on MBTI theory have a self-sorting section (not usually a formal questionnaire). Although none of these to my knowledge have been formally evaluated, elements of them are usually based on, or at least indirectly supported by, research findings.

Observational methods are a different approach. Five factor theory, which is associated with numerous paper-and-pencil self-report measures, has an observation form too (Costa and McCrae, 1992b). In agreement with Kenrick and Funder's (1988) classic paper on accuracy in person perception, they recommend obtaining ratings from those who are in a position to know the person being assessed well, for example partners and close colleagues. They also defend self-report questionnaires strongly. These do have considerable advantages: they work, and they're cheap and convenient.

In time (perhaps soon) I imagine we will have brain scanning ways of measuring type, or even a method using genetic testing. Brain scanning may also provide a way of measuring type development, but a battery of ability tests seems more likely.

4 Which other measures complement the MBTI questionnaire best?

FIRO-B and the Strong Interest Inventory may be used most often. However, I think that the MBTI questionnaire is usually used on its own, though not always with enough time allowed for interpreting or clarifying the results. For some purposes, an anxiety scale is the most obvious possibility.

5 Isn't type theory just like astrology?

MBTI theory and astrology have some things in common but one major difference: the quality of the evidence for MBTI theory, especially at the level of the preferences, compares well with the evidence for mainstream personality theories, while the quality of the evidence for astrology, from several thousand studies, is weak (see Dean 1986-7). Astrology has a fairly positive tone and a flexible, complicated conception of personality but appears to rely heavily on Barnum statements for its success. Barnum statements are personality descriptions which sound individual but are agreed with by a large proportion of people. For example, 'You have a tendency to be critical of yourself' and 'Security is one your major goals in life'. These make interesting reading both in themselves and when they are analysed from an MBTI perspective (Bayne, 2004).

Conclusions

The sustained success of MBTI theory and applications can be explained by its positive tone, its versatility and the evidence for its validity. 'Type' is a dangerous word but its strength is that it emphasizes first the fundamental nature of personality differences and second their structure within each person. The limitations of the theory are that it omits Anxiety, that type development is central to applications but not yet measured well, and that it is sometimes misused.

Evidence-based practice is obviously a good idea, but applying it is complicated. There are problems with producing the evidence, making it accessible to practitioners, and implementing it. Therefore, although practice needs to be guided by evidence as much as possible, the professional autonomy of practitioners remains central. It should be based on Pragmatic Science. The book is mainly concerned with applications of MBTI theory at the levels of the preferences and combinations of preferences, venturing occasionally into aspects of type dynamics.

MBTI theory and clarifying your own type (if you wish)

In this chapter I introduce MBTI theory in a way that allows you to assess your own psychological type if you wish, or to check the accuracy of an earlier assessment. You may also choose to assess other people's types instead of or as well as your own. The chapter is in four main sections:

1 Setting the scene, which discusses aspect of the process of observing and clarifying a person's psychological type, and the central concept of preference.

2 An introduction to the four pairs of preferences in MBTI theory. This is structured as a series of brief exercises and provisional decisions. It is a gathering of clues, detective work as emphasized in the first section.

3 Some further strategies for clarifying type and checking on judgements. This section includes two examples ('case' studies), a discussion of which are the best descriptions of the whole types, and an introduction to three other levels of MBTI theory: David Keirsey's temperament theory, type dynamics and type development. These other levels are introduced briefly, with two purposes in mind: their relevance to observing psychological type accurately enough to be useful and their use in particular applications in the rest of this book. The section ends with a discussion of ethical applications of the theory.

4 Replies (some in detail) to such questions as 'How many people of my type are there?' and 'Can type development be speeded up?'

Setting the scene

Generally, the best measure of psychological type is a combination of MBTI results and verifying them with a skilled practitioner. *You* decide how accurate your results are, at your own pace. For most people this is a fairly straightforward process. MBTI questionnaire results are accurate on average about 75 per cent of the time (Myers *et al.*, 1998) which means that for about 25 per cent of people, verification of MBTI results is *not* straightforward. This is *not* a sign of weakness or a flaw in the 25 per cent! Rather, it illustrates the great variety of human individuality. I've put two examples which make this point strongly in the third section, so that the section on assessing preferences can be fresh.

Assessments of a person's psychological type by others are generally valid too, though with scope for improvement (Bayne, 2004). These judgements of self and others should still be made with care which, in practice means approaching the judgements like a skilled and ethical detective.

'Detective work'

Carr (1997), who introduced the apt phrase 'detective work' (p. 1), is clear on what the detective work is for:

> Type clarification is a sifting process in which the practitioner tries to help the client to isolate their basic, enduring preferences from other influences on their behaviour.
>
> (Carr, 1997: 2)

Among the other influences on behaviour are:

- culture
- upbringing
- the situation (roles, other people)
- other personality characteristics
- mood
- stress
- type development

Some of the other factors which may interfere with accurate judgements of your preferences are:

- your self-image, e.g. of you as ideal woman, man, HRM professional, etc.
- influence from parents, guardians and others on how you *should* be

- the effects of stress
- type development

The central parallel between skilled 'detective work' and observing type accurately is looking for clues, and especially *patterns* of clues. Single clues are not enough. For example one of the clues for the JP preference is people's reactions to a deadline (exercise 2.1). I will discuss what JP means later in the chapter.

Exercise 2.1

Think about yourself and deadlines. Do you, circumstances allowing, like to start early or do you enjoy a surge of energy just before a deadline? Write down your thoughts. MBTI theory assumes that one of these reactions is *more* true of each person. There is some consistency, though perhaps not for everyone. If there isn't for you, please just accept it and continue.

A preference for J is associated with tending to start a piece of work early and, circumstances allowing, finishing it well before the deadline. This characteristic describes about 90 per cent of people with a preference for J (Quenk, Hammer and Majors, 2001).

Thus the remaining 10 per cent of Js behave like people with the opposite preference (for P) in this respect, though of course like Js in all or most other respects. This 10 per cent are called 'pressure-prompted Js', and they tend to do their best work at the last minute. Unfortunately for ease of accurate observation, behaving in a pressure-prompted way is characteristic of about 60 per cent of Ps, leaving 40 per cent of Ps as exceptions. Thus how someone reacts to deadlines is a useful clue for the JP preference but far from decisive. A lot more clues are needed to make an accurate judgement of preference for J or P.

Overall, it seems likely that accurate judgements of psychological type are based on several low-validity cues (but still valid) rather than a few highly valid ones. In addition, there are several biases working against accuracy, e.g. stereotypes and the primacy and recency effects (weighting either the first or the last clue observed too heavily). Remarkably, despite all the obstacles, most people observe personality fairly accurately (Kenrick and Funder, 1988; Bayne, 1995; Funder, 1995). Useful strategies for being more accurate are:

1 Treat first impressions as hypotheses, and look for patterns over time and across situations.
2 Look at *how* people do things and at what they're most and least enthusiastic about.
3 Look for evidence of motives.
4 Look for evidence *against* your first impressions, as well as for them.
5 Take situations into account. Some situations, e.g. selection interviews, first dates, lectures, tend to constrain behaviour much more than others.
6 Resist the temptation to interpret everything. Some behaviours have little or nothing to do with type.
7 Be clear about what you're looking for: about the concept of preference, and the characteristics associated with each preference.

Preference

Preference can be defined as 'feeling most natural and comfortable with a particular way of behaving and experiencing' (Bayne, 2004). Thus, someone with a preference for J will, given normal type development and the opportunities, behave in a J way *most* of the time and in a P way *some* of the time. We can do both, but we prefer one.

Exercise 2.2

Take a blank sheet of paper and write your normal signature. Next write your signature using your other hand. Write some adjectives describing the two experiences.

Some representative descriptions are:

Preferred hand	*Other hand*
Natural	Awkward
Comfortable	Clumsy
Easy	Childlike
Confident	Had to concentrate

Writing with your preferred hand is like behaving in tune with one of your preferences (in normal type development). Writing with your other hand is like using a non-preference.

The concept of preference, as applied to personality, makes sense to many people. It is embodied in everyday language, in such phrases as 'going against the grain' and 'it's my nature', though these phrases can mean quite different things in context and the term 'natural' can be a problem. I'll return to it in the final section. For the moment, it's an assumption in MBTI theory that preference is a useful idea and that it is defined in part by comfort and energy (Bayne, 2004).

Four pairs of preferences

Four preferences are distinguished in the theory. The first is Extraversion (E) versus Introversion (I). These terms are used broadly in MBTI theory, as much more than sociable and not sociable.

Exercise 2.3 Preference for E or I

Step 1   Think of someone you know who is more:

> Active than Reflective
> Sociable than Reserved
> Outgoing than Inward
> Centre of attention than Seeking the background

Keep in mind the idea of preference, as illustrated in the handedness exercise (2.2).
  These are clues for a preference for E.

Step 2   Think of someone you know who is more:

> Reflective than Active
> Reserved than Sociable
> Inward than Outgoing
> Seeking the background than Centre of attention

These are clues for I.

Step 3   Which – E or I – is most true of you? (Alternatively, which is *least* true of you? Sometimes it is easier to work backwards, to choose what is least comfortable and most effort.)

I'd like to re-emphasize that the clues for E and I in Exercise 2.3 are chosen from several possibilities and that your observations are provisional. Note too the positive language: all the terms are intended to describe generally desirable qualities, though inevitably some will be less appealing to some people.

If you can't decide between E and I, please just accept it and try the next exercise.

Exercise 2.4 **Preference for S or N**

Step 1 Think of someone you know who is more:

> Realistic than Imaginative
> Practical than Interested in theory
> Step by step than Leaping around (mentally)
> Interested in facts than the Big Picture

Keep in mind the idea of preference, as illustrated in the handedness exercise.

These are clues for a preference for Sensing (S).

Step 2 Think of someone you know who is more:

> Imaginative than Realistic
> Interested in theory than Practical
> Leaping around (mentally) than Step by step
> Interested in the Big Picture than Facts

These are clues for a preference for N (Intuition).

Step 3 Which – S or N – is most true of you? (Alternatively, which is *least* true of you? Your preference is, provisionally, the other letter.)

As a further check, try exercise 2.5.

Exercise 2.5

Read the following passages from an essay and write down your reactions. Is this person much like you – is there a shock of recognition – or not? Keep the notion of preference in mind. ▶

The writer has a clear and well-developed preference for Sensing and in the first passage she describes working as a florist.

One of the most enjoyable (if not profitable and feasible) jobs I have had was working as a florist. Even moving around the shop was a three dimensional experience in terms of the different scents from different flowers that I could pick out. It was very stimulating in terms of colours. And of course there was a huge tactile dimension in the contrasts between stems, petals, leaves, wrapping materials, terracotta, water, soil, ad infinitum. Some work I would do outside, some inside. And even within the shop there would be variations in lighting and temperature as I moved around from dim and cool storage areas, to direct sunlight in the windows and the artificially lit service areas.

In the second passage, the writer describes the effects of (for her) a much less positive working environment. It has implications for the health of people of her psychological type as well as for clarifying a preference for S or N.

When I have been working in an office I tend to eat substantially more, even though I am far more sedentary, and I think this is a result of the under stimulation I get from the office environment. In the office I handle only man-made materials, and largely computer keyboards and paper at that. The only variation in smell in the environment tends to be the air freshener in the toilets and if one of my clients is a bit pungent. The blinds, carpets, walls, computers are all grey and lit by fluorescent lighting. There is no variation in temperature through the day or even through the seasons. It is as a whole a very narrow world on a sensory level. People even bring me things to eat as they notice that I am always picking at something, to the extent that I am starting to notice that it is overcompensation with the sense of taste due to an absence of things for the other senses. The environment within which I work (and therefore spend a dominant proportion of my waking hours) is something that I am thinking about making a significant change to in the direction of something less flat and dull on a physical level.

I was struck by these examples of S because descriptions of S in the MBTI literature tend to be written by Ns, and to be described by Ss as 'pale' and inadequate. I don't think they would criticize these passages in the same way. A particular strength is that they're S in action, rather than writing about what it's like to be an S. On the other hand they are examples from the S of just one person to represent just one of the eight S types.

Exercise 2.6 **Preference for T or F**

Step 1 Think of someone you know who is more:

> Logical than Empathic
> Firm-minded than Warm-hearted
> Critical than Appreciative
> Analytic than Sympathetic

These are clues for a preference for Thinking (T). In making your choice, please note that Thinking is a technical term. It does *not* mean 'no emotions'.

Step 2 Think of someone you know who is more:

> Empathic than Logical
> Warm-hearted than Firm-minded
> Appreciative than Critical
> Sympathetic than Analytic

These are clues for a preference for Feeling (F). Feeling is a technical term which does *not* mean 'cannot think'.

Step 3 Which – T or F – is most true of you? (Alternatively, which is *least* true of you?)

Exercise 2.7 **Preference for J or P**

Step 1 Think of someone you know who is more:

> Organized than Easy-going
> Likes to have things settled than Open to alternatives
> Planful than Flexible

These are clues for Judging (J). Judging is a technical term which does *not* mean Judgemental. Take Exercise 2.1 on reactions to deadlines into account. ▶

> *Step 2*   Think of someone you know who is more:
>
> > Easy-going than Organized
> > Open to alternatives than Likes to have things settled
> > Flexible than Planful
>
> These are clues for Perceiving (P).
>
> *Step 3*   Which – J or P – is most true of you? (Alternatively, which is *least* true of you?)

At this point I hope you will have a beginning idea about each of the four preferences and, if you chose to assess yourself, a *provisional* decision about your own psychological type or part of it.

Type

In MBTI theory, your 'type' consists of four letters – your preference in each of the four pairs above. Thus you might have chosen ESFJ or, if there was not enough information or clarity for you, perhaps one, two or three of the preferences, leaving the other(s) open. There are sixteen possible combinations of the preferences and therefore sixteen types. However, I have come across a few people who seemed, to themselves and to me, equally comfortable with both preferences in a pair and who described themselves as say both ENTJ and INTJ. Whether they are best described as two types or as one type with excellent development of a non-preference is arguable. For one person to be equally all sixteen types or even four types seems to me very unlikely.

A note on the positive tone of MBTI descriptions

MBTI theory and five factor theory (and other major theories) differ markedly in tone. Thus, in contrast to the preferences, the factors in five factor theory tend to have a positive and a negative end. For example, people high on Conscientiousness (the parallel in MBTI theory is J) are described, among other qualities, as 'well-organized' and 'self-disciplined' while those scoring low are 'weak-willed' and 'careless'.

The parallel in MBTI theory to low Conscientiousness is P and, as illustrated earlier, it is described in terms like 'flexible' and 'adaptable'. This difference of interpretation and tone has significant effects, some of which are discussed later, in Chapters 4 (selection) and 8 (counselling and coaching). Another example is scoring low on the factor of Agreeableness (the MBTI parallel is T). Typical five factor theory adjectives are 'ruthless' and 'suspicious'. Typical MBTI theory adjectives are 'firm-minded' and 'critical' (in a largely positive sense).

A major general effect of this difference in tone is that MBTI theory is much more useful than five factor theory in organizations. It does recognize weaknesses in its theory of development, but is more even-handed and suggests a wider range of strengths.

Clarifying type: further strategies and perspectives

There are several strategies for clarifying or verifying type. I have tried to incorporate some of them into the step-by-step process earlier in this chapter. Carr (1997) provides an excellent practical discussion of most of the strategies, including the most bold and direct: behaving like a type you suspect you might be for a few hours or days. In this section, I discuss three further strategies and perspectives on type clarification: case studies, descriptions of the types and three other levels of MBTI theory.

Two examples

Sally Carr also describes her clarification of her own psychological type. Her MBTI results were ENTP which, she writes, 'seemed a reasonable enough fit. However, it never seemed to do anything for me or help me to understand my reactions' (p. 20). This lukewarm reaction isn't the kind of confirmation hoped for! The doubtful element was SN. She resolved it by talking it through with a colleague, and discovering that she believed that N was better in the sense of superior. Both her family and her training as an occupational psychologist were sources of this belief, and she had indeed become quite adept with complex theories (an N skill and therefore, in an S type, an example of developing a non-preference).

Another good clue to her true preference for S was the way she worked on understanding theories through specific examples. 'If I could not do this, I would find the concepts frustrating and meaningless.' In addition, she realized that she'd never fully valued her S abilities, 'tending to feel that if something comes easily, it couldn't be worth very much' (p. 21). This illustrates the effort/energy/comfort criterion for a true preference.

Sally therefore tried out ESTP for 'fit', a decision that was 'associated with an immediate rush of excitement and energy, as seems to be characteristic of people discovering their true preferences' (p. 21). (I think it would be interesting to know if it's more true of SPs than other types). For Sally, the result was 'a sense of release and new freedom to enjoying aspects of myself which I had tended to undervalue'.

My own experience also started with inaccurate MBTI results – but the questionnaire really does seem to be accurate for about 75 per cent of people (Myers *et al.*, 1998). My recollection and my approach to clarification is much less analytic and detailed than Sally's, and thus equally true to type. My results were INTJ. An ISTJ close friend was very clear that IN was accurate for me and that TJ wasn't. My response, which I was happy with for over a year, was that she was a more clearcut TJ than me, but that I was still a TJ. This was partly because I liked the INTJ description best; partly lack of understanding of the theory (I had given myself the MBTI and there were no courses or workshops then – it was about 1982, and very few people in the UK were trained); partly because I was so pleased with the IN elements; and partly because of my real type (INFPs tend to be less sceptical than INTJs). During the year, I tried out INFJ briefly but then, for no particular reason, decided my friend was right. I'm still sure, over twenty years later.

Some implications of these two examples for clarifying type are to take your time, to seek out several sources of evidence (perhaps perceptive friends in particular) and to participate in a workshop if possible. I think workshops are more effective than one-to-one feedback (Bayne, 2004).

Which are the best descriptions of the types?

Another strategy is to read descriptions of each type, or of each of the types you're considering. This raises the question of which of the many sets of descriptions are the most accurate (Bayne, 2004). The answer may be complicated, e.g. the best ISFP description might be in one set and the best ESTJ description in another.

The most creative attempt to describe the sixteen types so far is by Berens and Nardi (1999). They offer three formats: brief 'snapshot', third person and first person. The first-person portraits are composites from interviews with at least four people of each type. Berens and Nardi recommend considering all three formats together and find that each works best for some people. This seems to me a significant attempt to improve descriptions of the types and one that in the self-portraits is partly empirical. However, it would be useful to know, as with all the other descriptions, which aspects of their snapshots, portraits and self-portraits work best generally and which with particular kinds of people. In addition, there are some *possible* Barnum statements in the Berens and Nardi descriptions. These are descriptions of aspects of personality which seem individual but are actually true of most people, e.g. 'They often instantly like people or not' and 'They often feel a strong need to discover a definitive direction for themselves' (p. 40).

The descriptions in the sixth edition of *Introduction to Type* (Myers with Kirby and K. Myers, 1998) were compiled and validated as follows, and therefore are probably the best currently available:

1 Descriptions from Myers' earlier attempts and five MBTI books were compiled into a questionnaire.
2 The questionnaire was completed by groups of five or six people of each type who had verified their types but weren't experienced with type, and sent to about thirty experts on type for comment.
3 The results were combined with ratings of descriptions from several studies.
4 The highest-rated descriptions were used in *Introduction to Type* after a further consultation with people of each type.
5 The descriptions were organized into the following sections: each type at its best; how others may see them; and potential areas for growth. The 'areas for growth' describe typical behaviour resulting from
  • not developing the dominant or auxiliary (see later section, on type dynamics, in this chapter)
  • not being able to express their type
  • neglecting their non-preferences too much
  • being under great stress

These descriptions have therefore been developed carefully, thoroughly and logically. Other, freer, more speculative descriptions have, however, proved crucial for some people in clarifying their type, e.g. those in the early editions of *Introduction to Type*, Keirsey and Bates (1973), Kroeger and Thuesen (1988), Hirsh and Kummerow (2000), DiTiberio and Hammer (1993) and Lawrence (1998).

Temperament theory (Keirsey)

Although MBTI theory is quite complicated, one of its strengths is that several simpler levels of description can be useful, the simplest of all being one of the pairs of preferences in isolation. At an intermediate level of complexity, Keirsey and Bates (1973; Keirsey, 1998) suggested four 'temperaments', each identified by two preferences. For example, NF includes INFP, INFJ, ENFP and ENFJ.

Exercise 2.8

Step 1   Can you think of someone who fits each temperament as depicted in the stick figures and the list of core motives below?

Step 2   Rank the four stick figures from most like you to least like you. (You may find it easier to start with 'least like'.)

I see the following summary of the core motives as *relatively* important in each temperament, e.g. everyone needs some excitement (SP) and some stability (SJ), but is one of them *more* characteristic of the particular person or of you? Much more strongly, ask: 'Are there any that are so central to me that for them to be blocked would be like "psychological death"' (Berens, 2000 p. 24). And 'Are there any that you're relatively indifferent to?'.

SP   Excitement; solving practical problems; freedom (e.g. from planning in detail); variety.

SJ   Being responsible and useful; stability; planning in detail.

NT   Developing new methods/theories/models/a grand vision; analysing and criticizing.

NF   Self-development; supporting other people; harmony; authenticity.

Figure 2.1 | **Typical SP characteristics © OKA (Otto Kroeger Associates)**

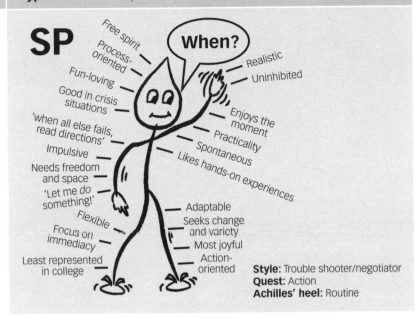

Figure 2.2 | **Typical SJ characteristics © OKA (Otto Kroeger Associates)**

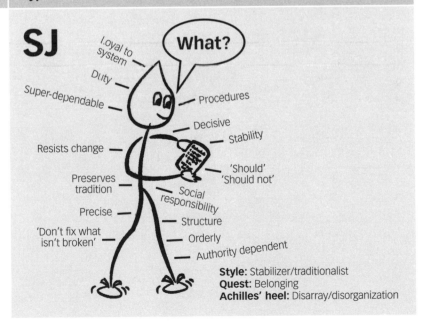

Figure 2.3 | **Typical NT characteristics © OKA (Otto Kroeger Associates)**

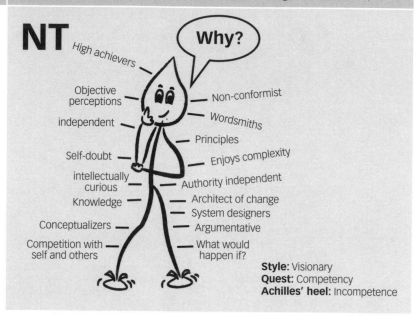

Figure 2.4 | **Typical NF characteristics © OKA (Otto Kroeger Associates)**

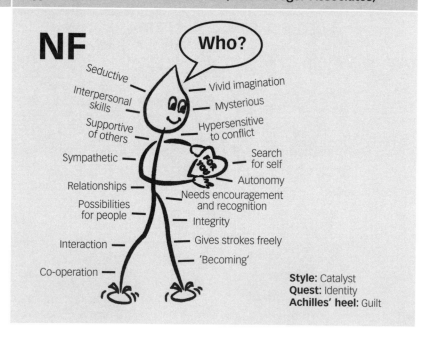

Keirsey's temperament theory is treated in two distinct ways in the MBTI literature, as one of the most practical and powerful levels of MBTI theory (e.g. Kroeger and Thuesen, 1998), or as a theory in its own right (e.g. Berens, 1999). I'm treating it here mainly as a further source of clues to your own type. If your judgements of preferences and temperament agree with each other (e.g. ENFP and NF), that's obviously clearer than if they don't. If they disagree, then more thought or more clues are needed to clarify your type. However, the stick figures haven't been formally evaluated, and the adjectives used in the preference exercises have.

Two other strategies are to take type dynamics, and type development into account. These levels of type theory are discussed briefly next.

Type dynamics

The main idea in type dynamics is that one of the four functions (S, N, T and F) is dominant, another auxiliary and so on, and that if someone doesn't use their dominant function sufficiently, and more than other functions, they are unlikely to feel fulfilled or at their best. Thus, in normal type development, the dominant function 'plays by far the biggest role in the personality' (Lawrence, 1997, p. 11). The characteristics associated with it are the most characteristic qualities of a person. A second idea is that the fourth function, which is the opposite of the dominant, is likely to be the least developed, again with consequences for behaviour (Myers, K. and Kirby, 1998; Quenk, 2002).

The dominant functions and fourth functions of each type are as follows:

	Dominant	Fourth
ISTJ, ISFJ, ESTP, ESFP	S	N
INTJ, INFJ, ENTP, ENFP	N	S
ISTP, INTP, ESTJ, ENTJ	T	F
ISFP, INFP, ESFJ, ENFJ	F	T

Thus, statements about characteristics associated with each preference apply *most* to a person's dominant function (S, N, T or F) and *least* to their fourth function. The auxiliary or second function in each type is the preference for S, N, T or F which is not the dominant. For example in ISTJs it's T and in ENFPs, it's F. In terms of an organizational analogy, the auxiliary is the 'personal secretary' to the dominant function's MD. At another level of MBTI theory, EI plays a part too, because each dominant and auxiliary function is either extraverted or introverted (Thompson, 1996a), but the version described above is sufficient for the purposes of this book.

Two other ideas in type dynamics are worth noting here. First, it's suggested that each of us can become 'gripped' by our fourth function (the opposite of our dominant) especially when we are tired, ill or very stressed. The fourth function expresses itself as an immature under-developed form of the preference.

For example, someone in the grip of T will be one or more of the following:

- very critical of self or others (feeling useless, incompetent)
- analysing compulsively (and with a strange energy)
- immobilized

The other functions are thought to express themselves in the grip as follows:

F   Have an emotional outburst and be startled or frightened by it and the way it seems to take over. Feel attacked, wounded, violated or unloved – that no-one cares. Thinking about emotions – the most natural strategy for someone whose dominant function is T – is sometimes not effective, e.g. doesn't lead to control.

S   Overdo something tangible, e.g. overeat, count compulsively, make lots of lists.

N   See only gloomy possibilities and feel trapped.

Second, the basic motives for each dominant function (cf. those for the temperaments) are:

For S, to have real, practical experiences.
For N, to find exciting possibilities.
For T, to create logical order.
For F, to live harmoniously.

These are very general statements and also the simplest variation (cf. Myers, K. and Kirby, 1994). They do seem to be useful but, like the ideas about the fourth function, the evidence for them is mainly anecdotal and *could* simply be the result of biased observation and selective memory (Bayne, 2004).

Type development

Type theory assumes that equal development of all the functions is not desirable: that the dominant function should be the most developed function, the auxiliary the second most developed in each type, and so on. It also assumes that equal development rarely happens because it's not possible to be interested in, for example, both what is happening (S) and in possibilities (N) at the same time and that this tends to lead to one preference being used more, trusted more and more developed, and so on, in a cumulative and spiral process. Meanwhile, the other preference is relatively shut off, neglected and undeveloped. A firm sense of self or identity seems to require this kind of consistency which then acts as an 'anchor' for a person's identity. There are considerable individual differences in how many preferences are developed, to what extent and when.

Good development further assumes that balance in another sense, between different kinds of function, is desirable:

> The need for such supplementing is obvious. Perception without judgement is spineless; judgement with no perception is blind. Introversion lacking any extraversion is impractical; extraversion with no introversion is superficial.
>
> (Myers with Myers, 1980 p. 182).

This need for a balance between the perceiving function (S and N) and the judging functions (T and F), and between E and I, seems feasible too: everyone takes in information and comes to conclusions about it and everyone behaves introvertedly sometimes and extravertedly at other times.

The general picture in normal type development is of each person gradually discovering what they are best at – their talents, gift and central motives – and what is 'not them'. We then spend more time and energy on what we are best at and necessarily less on other things.

There's only so much time and energy, especially when using a non-preference.

A further suggestion is that development of the dominant and auxiliary, at least in some people, reaches a kind of ceiling and then more attention is paid to the third and fourth functions (in this order). For example, some ENFPs, who have been primarily imaginative and enthusiastic, do not become ISTJs but do reach a time when they find reflection, logic, analysis and/or planning more attractive (Myers with Myers, 1980; Provost, 1993; Myers, K. and Kirby, 1994). Judy Provost (1993, p. 7) suggests that 'If and when No. 4 (and No. 3) can be utilized in mature adulthood, the outcome is often positive, even exhilarating'. I suspect that this is true more often for some types (ENPs?) than others and that some mature adults do not develop their third or fourth preferences to the extent Provost suggests, despite opportunity, but become more and more like their types.

There is only a little research on type development and hardly any theory about the third function. The fourth function, as indicated earlier, is much speculated about: it can be seen as a part of ourselves we tend to 'confront' in midlife, as something we mostly avoid but can be 'hooked' by, that can attack us, fascinate us and sometimes 'spins us around' (Jung, 1923, para. 85).

If a true preference is actively discouraged for long enough (type theory seems to see the preferences as sufficiently robust to resist lack of encouragement), then a false type develops. For Jung and Myers, the consequences for the individual are less effective behaviour, a sense of 'not being right' and possibly acute exhaustion and neurosis (Jung, 1923, paras 560–1).

It is easy to picture environmental factors that can impede or suppress type development: a T child who is not allowed to argue, an I who is not allowed time alone, an S who is expected to learn only through reading. These examples confound two processes: discouraging the child from using their natural preferences and encouraging them (probably with love and good intentions) to use their non-preferences. Myers refers to falsification of type, 'a process which robs its victims of their real selves and makes them into inferior, frustrated copies of other people' (1980, p. 189). Various patterns of type development are possible, e.g. initially developing the functions in a different order from the one proposed by the theory but later in life recovering to the 'right' order.

Now that I've introduced MBTI theory, and before turning to specific areas of application, I'd like to emphasize some aspects of ethical application.

Ethical application of MBTI theory

The main danger in MBTI practice is bias. It can be blatant or subtle, as can unfair discrimination in other respects. The following two examples of 'type-bashing' illustrate blatant bias. The first is from Kummerow (2001). A speaker at a conference says she needs to explain an intuitive leap to people in the audience who prefer Sensing. Kummerow commented: 'Why single out sensing types ... Why not just say something inclusive like, "Let me explain my intuitive leap ... Then the focus could have been on the fun of the association, not the alleged stupidity of sensing types for not leaping regularly' (p. 8).

The ethical principle here is about recognising, accepting and valuing difference, rather than excluding and stereotyping a whole group of people. In the same spirit, Kummerow suggests saying inclusive things like 'This is an opportunity for everyone to use their introverted side,' rather than 'I know it will be hard for Es to be quiet!'

The second example of blatant bias is an advert in the BPS Appointments Bulletin for an organizational psychologist which stated that 'ESTJs and people who do not know what that means need not apply.' The point here, just to be really clear, is that the best applicant might be an ESTJ with good development of her or his non-preferences. Asking for knowledge of MBTI theory was a much more defensible criterion.

A more subtle example of bias is that there's a difference between saying 'I'm doing this because I'm a P and that tends to be how I express P' (ethical version) and 'I'm doing this because that's what Ps do' (stereotypical version). The difference is that the stereotypical version implies that *all* Ps do this (and *no* Js), and that's not the case. It may also be using type as an excuse, which is another kind of ethical error, e.g. 'You can't expect me to be on time, I'm a P.'

Overall, I agree with Lawrence and Martin (2001) when they say that 'ethical use and skilful use of the MBTI are the same thing' (p. 175).

Questions and replies

1 How many people of my type are there?

The data on the proportions of people of each type in the UK (Table 2.1) were collected from a representative sample of the general population by the Office of National Statistics (Kendall, 1998, p. 60). I have simplified them here by eliminating fractions; it's less cluttered to say that 2 per cent of people are INTJs as it is to say 2.2 per cent. A cost is that these approximate percentages don't always add up to 100 per cent. The only other country so far with such good information on incidence is the US (Table 2.2).

The figures in Table 2.1 and 2.2 aren't perfect. For example, these are MBTI types rather than verified types and an analysis of clear scores only would be interesting since as Walck (1992) and others have shown, they are much more likely to indicate true types. In addition, people who don't answer questionnaires or who have severe mental health problems, are under-represented. If type is related to any of these characteristics, then the samples are not representative.

In the two samples the incidence of the preferences (in percentages) is as follows:

	UK	US
E	53	49
I	47	51
S	76	74
N	24	28
T	46	57
F	54	43
J	58	54
P	42	46

There is only one substantial gender difference in the preferences, on TF. It is probably the largest psychological difference of any kind, apart from some aspects of sexuality, between the sexes, but nevertheless there is also a large overlap. The difference is of course consistent with

Table 2.1	**MBTI types (%s) in a representative sample of 1,634 UK adults**

ISTJ	ISFJ	INFJ	INTJ
14	13	2	1
ISTP	**ISFP**	**INFP**	**INTP**
6	6	**3**	2
ESTP	**ESFP**	**ENFP**	**ENTP**
6	9	6	3
ESTJ	**ESFJ**	**ENFJ**	**ENTJ**
10	13	3	3

Source: Modified from Kendall (1998) p. 57
Modified and reproduced by special permission from CPP, Inc., Palo Alto, CA 94303 from Myers-Briggs Type Indicator European Edition Manual Supplement by Elizabeth Kendall. Copyright 1998 by Peter B. Myers and Katharine D. Myers. All rights reserved. Further reproduction is prohibited without prior written consent from CPP, Inc.

Table 2.2	**MBTI types (%s) in a representative sample of 3,009 US adults.**

ISTJ	ISFJ	INFJ	INTJ
12	13	3	2
ISTP	**ISFP**	**INFP**	**INTP**
5	8	4	3
ESTP	**ESFP**	**ENFP**	**ENTP**
4	8	8	3
ESTJ	**ESFJ**	**ENFJ**	**ENTJ**
8	12	2	2

Source: Modified from Myers *et al.* (1998, pp. 157–8)
Modified and reproduced by special permission of the publisher, CPP Inc., Palo Alto, CA 94303 from *MBTI Manual: A Guide to the Development and Use of the Myers-Briggs Type Indicator*, Third Edition by Isabel Briggs Myers, Mary H. McCaulley, Naomi L. Quenk and Allen L. Hammer. Copyright 1998 by CPP Inc. All rights reserved. Further reproduction is prohibited without the Publisher's written consent.

social stereotypes (and therefore pressures), and this *may* mean that the real difference is less or even does not exist, but there's no evidence for this. The approximate figures are:

	UK		US	
	Male	Female	Male	Female
T	65	30	57	24
F	35	70	44	76

Other points from Tables 2.1 and 2.2 are the roughly equal proportions of Es and Is when early US estimates were 3:1 Es to Is, and the 3:1 ratio of Ss to Ns.

The percentages of each temperament (in Keirsey's sense), again approximate, are:

	SP	SJ	NT	NF
UK	27	51	9	14
US	25	43	10	16

Gender differences in the types in UK and US general population samples are shown in Tables 2.3 and 2.4.

2 Isn't personality more a social construction?

The constructionist view is that personality doesn't really exist; it's a perception constructed by the observer. (More generally, it's the view that objective reality doesn't exist either.) I think it was demolished in Kenrick and Funder's (1988) review of the research on accuracy in person perception. The evidence of genetic influences on personality (and/or anything else) also seems to me to support a realist position.

Table 2.3 **MBTI types (%s) by gender (865 UK female, 748 UK male adults)**

	ISTJ		ISFJ		INFJ		INTJ
M	20	M	7	M	2	M	3
F	9	F	18	F	2	F	1
	ISTP		**ISFP**		**INFP**		**INTP**
M	11	M	4	M	4	M	4
F	3	F	8	F	3	F	1
	ESTP		**ESFP**		**ENFP**		**ENTP**
M	8	M	6	M	5	M	4
F	4	F	11	F	8	F	2
	ESTJ		**ESFJ**		**ENFJ**		**ENTJ**
M	12	M	6	M	2	M	4
F	10	F	19	F	3	F	2

Source: Modified from Kendall (1998 pp. 58 – 9)

Table 2.4	**MBTI types (%s) by gender (1,478 US male, 1,531 US female adults)**			
	ISTJ	**ISFJ**	**INFJ**	**INTJ**
	M 16	M 8	M 1	M 3
	F 7	F 19	F 2	F 1
	ISTP	**ISFP**	**INFP**	**INTP**
	M 9	M 8	M 4	M 5
	F 2	F 10	F 5	F 2
	ESTP	**ESFP**	**ENFP**	**ENTP**
	M 6	M 7	M 6	M 4
	F 3	F 10	F 10	F 2
	ESTJ	**ESFJ**	**ENFJ**	**ENTJ**
	M 11	M 8	M 2	M 3
	F 6	F 17	F 3	F 1

Source: Modified from Myers *et al.* (1998, pp. 157–8)
Modified and reproduced by special permission from CPP, Inc., Palo Alto, CA 94303 from *MBTI Manual: A Guide to the Development and Use of the Myers-Briggs Type Indicator*, Third Edition by Isabel Briggs Myers, Mary H. McCaulley, Naomi L. Quenk and Allen L. Hammer. Copyright 1998 by CPP Inc. All rights reserved. Further reproduction is prohibited without the Publisher's written consent.

3 Is there really a 'real self'? And what does 'natural' mean?

There are problems with both 'real' and 'natural' but they are indispensable in several personality theories (Bayne, 1995). 'Naturally' is the subtext in the exercises on the preferences and temperaments earlier in this chapter.

I find Costa and McCrae's (1992a) analysis of the related concept of 'basic' helpful. They suggest four criteria of basic personality characteristics: that self-ratings and ratings by other are highly correlated and stable over several years; that they are pervasive; that they are found in different age groups and a wide variety of cultures; and that there is evidence of genetic influences. Each of these criteria is met by the five factors and therefore by the four preferences.

4 Is type genetic?

The first point to make is that MBTI theory is useful whether type has a genetic element or not. Second, even identical twins differ in personality although they share the same DNA. Chance plays a role here and in development generally.

I think MBTI theory assumes a genetic predisposition for the preferences which are then encouraged or suppressed to varying degrees by the environment, and that there is strong evidence to support this view. The most dramatic evidence comes from identical twins being separated early, growing up in different environments (sometimes very different), and yet being much more similar in personality than children brought up in the same environment. Indeed, identical twins brought up apart are about as similar as those brought up together in contrast to adopted (and therefore genetically unrelated) children brought up together who are very unlike each other – as, much of the time, are siblings of course.

Another line of research is genetics itself, e.g. Plomin's (2001, p. 137) view is that: 'Genes responsible for the heritability of personality are beginning to be identified.' He also uses the vivid terms 'appetites' and 'vulnerabilities' for what is inherited. They imply that it's a matter of nature *and* nurture, rather than inborn *versus* learned. As Isabel Myers puts it in *Gifts Differing*: '. . . the successful development of type can be greatly helped or hindered by environment from the beginning' (Myers with Myers, 1980, p. 176).

On a more formal level, the leading personality journals have published numerous papers on personality and genetics over the last few years. For example, Loehlin *et al.* (1998), using a sample of over 800 pairs of twins, stated that 'The Big Five' dimensions, which are closely related to four of the MBTI preferences, 'are substantially and about equally heritable, with little or no contribution of shared family environment' (p. 431).

However, there's much more to this question, which is discussed in a sophisticated and clear way by Steven Pinker in *The Blank Slate* (2002) and Jay Joseph in *The Gene Illusion* (2003), and in relation to MBTI theory by Bayne (2004).

5 Can your type change?

It depends on what you mean by 'type' and 'change'. MBTI theory says that each of us remains one type throughout our lives but that we gradually develop both our preferences and our non-preferences. A major change occurs when someone discards a 'false' type or preference.

6 How different are people of the same type?

They can be very different, depending on such factors as type development (including type falsification), culture, other personality characteristics and situations.

7 Is everyone a type?

Some people's types are, at the very least, hard to judge, either by themselves or others. I think it's pragmatic and respectful to accept that a few people are genuinely two or perhaps four types and the way genes influence behaviour is consistent with this (Pinker, 2002). The main problem is at the level of personality structure, e.g. would the person have two dominant functions?

8 Is there a difference between your type at work and at home?

Not when the preferences are defined as 'stable underlying dispositions'. There may be significant differences in behaviour in the two situations. Moreover, the MBTI questionnaire may generally be answered more accurately when thinking of oneself at home rather than at work. Again, comfort and whether or not you feel free to express your type are central.

9 Can type development be speeded up, and should it be speeded up?

One answer to this question is 'Yes, when there has been false type development.' But the main sense of this question is whether, in normal development, it is desirable to 'forcefeed' a natural process. If there is normal type development, it may be best to let it continue to happen at its own pace. One possible disadvantage of conscious attempts to speed up development is feeling pressured to be perfect or, of course, developing 'too fast' and missing out on what may be the intrinsic pleasures of developing at a 'natural' pace. However, some conscious intent and action to develop one's type may be a reasonable and attractive option.

A further consideration is that logic (yet to be tested by research) suggests that significant development of E, I, J and P is more basic than development of S, N, T and F. It hardly seems possible to live without developing some E (though Es may perhaps manage better without I) and being only J or P would similarly be too extreme a handicap. Things would be done too quickly or nothing would be finished. In contrast, some people seem to cope fairly well without obvious development of one or two of S, N, T and F though there are of course consequences for themselves and others. At some point (theoretically, midlife) pressures from within and from life events might demand some attention for the neglected preferences.

10 How might type development be speeded up?

Some strategies for developing EI and JP are:

E   Speak spontaneously
    Talk to an audience
    Introduce yourself to someone you don't know

I   Spend undistracted time alone
    Stay quiet in a group
    Work alone on a project

J   Make a list of things to do, put them in order of priority, and do
       the first one
    Make a plan and stick to it

P   Spend unplanned time following impulses
    Re-examine a final decision

And for SN and TF:

S   Observe something carefully, e.g. non-verbal behaviour (E),
       nature (E), your inner physical state (I)
    Eat slowly and with concentration (I)
    Massage (EI), dance (E), housework (E)
    Do anything that requires attention to detail (E)
    List all the facts about something (E)
    Compare your facts with an S's*
    Describe an activity, step by step (E)
    Compare your description with an S's*

N   Brainstorm (I)
Compare your brainstorm with an N's*
Focus on the 'big picture' (E)
Compare your big picture with an N's*
Daydream or fantasize (I)
Imagine five years ahead (I)
Travel to new countries (E)

T   Devise a flowchart (I)
Ask a T to critique it*
List the costs and benefits of a decision (I)
Ask a T for their's*
Tell someone what you find difficult about them (E)
Define something precisely (I)
Ask a T for their definition*

F   Clarify your values (I)
Ask an F for their's*
Empathize (E)
Use more emotion words in writing or speaking (I)
Compliment someone on their appearance or personality (E)
List things you like and dislike (I)

The (E)s and (I)s indicate extraverted and introverted variations of SN and TF, a level of MBTI theory mentioned briefly in the earlier section on type dynamics (e.g. Thompson, 1996a). The *s indicate my belief that we tend to overestimate our skill in the attributes associated with our non-preferences and suggest ways of testing this.

Your reactions to these strategies for type development or to the prospect of them (and to the MBTI holidays in Chapter 3) are of course further clues to your psychological type but – and I think this is a recognition of real complexity rather than 'cheating' – a positive reaction may alternatively indicate a non-preference pressing for expression.

11 How can I find a reputable MBTI course/practitioner?

In the UK and Europe:

OPP   BAPT
www.opp.co.uk   *www.bapt*

Phone: 01865 404 500

In the US:

CAPT
www.capt.org

Phone: 800 777 2278

APT

Australia, New Zealand, France, Japan, Korea, Latin America, Singapore and South Africa currently (August 2003) have Associations for Psychological Type (APTs). For details, see *www.aptcentral.org*

Conclusions

In MBTI theory and applications, clarifying a person's psychological type is a step towards understanding their individuality rather than an attempt to capture and tame it. The process is like skilled detective work, especially in its search for patterns of clues and for evidence for and against each hypothesis. The chapter sets the scene for clarifying type in a provisional and respectful way. At the same time it introduces MBTI theory, particularly the four pairs of preferences.

The best descriptions of the types so far are probably in the sixth edition of *Introduction to Type*, but other longer, freer descriptions have proved crucial for some people. More speculative levels of MBTI theory can also be very helpful. Temperament theory is a simpler level. Type dynamics and type development are deeper, enriching levels. The main ethical risk in applying the theory is bias through stereotyping. Skilful application reduces this risk.

3   Careers

How many people are in work that suits them? Surveys which attempt to measure 'job satisfaction' suggest that most people are satisfied (Doyle, 2003). MBTI theory suggests that job satisfaction and job performance go together, and mainstream theories (e.g. Schein, 1993; Holland, 1996) agree. For example, Holland writes:

> It is assumed – other things being equal – that congruence of person and job environment leads to job satisfaction, stability of career path, and achievement. Conversely, incongruence (i.e. person and job are mismatched) leads to dissatisfaction, instability of career path, and low performance.
>
> (1996, p. 397)

However, there are problems with and qualifications of these ideas and findings. First, 'satisfaction' is such a bland word. What about fulfilment or excitement? Second, even if the findings about job satisfaction are broadly true, they do leave room for improvement. Third, good evidence for the assumed link between satisfaction and effectiveness is not available (Doyle, 2003), though this may be explained by difficulties of measurement. Fourth, there are contrasting views, e.g. Studs Terkel introduced his book *Working* as follows:

> This book, being about work, is, by its very nature, about violence – to the spirit as well as to the body. It is about ulcers as well as accidents, about shouting matches as well as fistfights, about nervous breakdown as well as kicking the dog around. It is, above all, about daily humiliations.
>
> (1972, p. xi)

How many people would agree with Studs Terkel today? There *are* some reports of widespread dissatisfaction. For example, Marcus

Buckingham (2001) reported that interviews of a national UK sample of employees using twelve 'powerful questions', found that only 17 per cent were psychologically 'engaged' at work, with 63 per cent 'not engaged' and 20 per cent 'actively disengaged'. 'Engaged' was defined as being loyal and productive, and disengaged employees missed more days work and were much more expensive in other ways too. Another stimulating finding was that 'all cultures are local' (p. 40) – large organizations don't have a single culture but a very varied one, created by the behaviour of local managers and teams (through clarity of expectations, strength of relationships, etc.).

Examples of the questions used in Buckingham's research, which are much more demanding than 'How satisfied are you with your work?', are:

- At work, do I have the opportunity to do what I do best every day?
- In the past seven days, have I received recognition or praise for good work?
- In the past six months, have I talked to someone about my progress?
- Does my supervisor, or someone at work, seem to care about me as a person?

In the rest of this chapter I discuss four aspects of psychological type and careers:

1 The notions of a 'career' and of people finding careers that 'suit' them, obstacles to such matching and more holistic (postmodern) approaches to 'career';
2 career choice;
3 job satisfaction, job performance and retention;
4 improving the process of searching for a fulfilling career.

The idea of a career

The idea of a career can be seen as a key notion in twentieth-century Western societies (Young and Collin, 2000; Bimrose *et al.*, 2003). Young and Collin (2000) suggest a wide range of meanings of 'career'. These include career as a construct used in organizations to motivate and persuade employees; as a construct embracing attitudes and behaviours associated with work over a lifetime; and as a construct involving self-identity, hopes, dreams, fears and frustrations. Overall, they suggest that 'career can be seen as an overreaching construct that gives meaning to the individual's life' (p. 5). Myers (1977) expressed a similar idea very strongly: 'Probably nothing can enhance your life more than having the kind of work you really love, that makes you feel alive' (p. 4).

Several other factors influence the careers we actually find ourselves in: availability (sometimes the problem is to find any work at all, and the idea of a career or career choice is a joke); luck; advice; abilities; values; and interests. Some factors (e.g. racism and sexism) impede or prevent good matches between people and careers (Bimrose *et al.*, 2003). Martin (1995) and Tieger and Barron-Tieger (2001), the two key books on type and careers, both include sections on values and interests. I think interests related to type are also indicated in the 'MBTI holidays' (Box 3.1), and that they're good clues to type as well as to interests (Bayne, 2004).

Box 3.1	**MBTI holidays**	
	ISTJ	Gourmet's tour of France, savouring the delights of traditional vineyards (and grape crushing by foot), specialist fromageries and local cuisine.
	ISTP	Driving a modern, high-tech, all-amenities camper van around America's National Parks, with the freedom to experience the natural beauty in your own way.
	ESTP	White water rafting, bungee jumping and crocodile wrestling in Oz.
	ESTJ	Visiting Disneyland with the family, getting up at dawn to be the first in the queue, 'doing' it all before it gets busy and then leaving to fit in another attraction before tea time.
	ISFJ	A well-earned week away with your true love in a Grade 2 listed building, sifting through the local antique shops.
	ISFP	Walking in Provence, experiencing the local culture, staying with local families, visiting markets and eating local cuisine.
	ESFP	Driving an old fashioned VW camper van to a rally with all the family, and having cook-outs with a large group of like-minded people. ▶

ESFJ	Italian cookery in Tuscany with practical lessons each morning, convivial lunches getting to know other course members and time to visit local sites and relax with new friends in the afternoons.
INFJ	The long-planned romantic week away in a rustic, rose-covered cottage in Dorset. Taking the Labrador for long walks with your significant other, and cosy evenings sipping wine in front of the log fire.
INFP	Being alone with the elements to find yourself and meditate; exploring the coastline of NW Greenland at your own pace.
ENFP	Staying in a large country house with a horde of friends, having extended discussions, playing games, and having many activities to choose from.
ENFJ	Spiritual retreat on a Greek island, exploring new techniques of self-actualization with a group of soul mates.
INTJ	Visiting Boston to take a crash course in quantum mechanics at MIT.
INTP	Visiting the Leonardo Museum in Vinci, staying in perfect, individual accommodation, perhaps in a room once occupied by a famous scientist.
ENTP	Backpacking around the Middle East with the option of side trips to Turkey, Egypt and Milan, learning about the local cultures, creating stories to tell all your friends when you get home.
ENTJ	Getting away from the pressures of work with a two-week intensive MBA course in a city where everything is happening.

Exercise 3.1

Step 1 Do the holidays give you any possible insights relevant to choice of career?

Step 2 Are the insights (if any) related to your psychological type?

A related way of clarifying genuine interests, which it can be very difficult to be sure of, is to look at an array of magazines: which would you read on a journey or in a waiting room? One of the difficulties is expressed well in the MBTI *Manual*: 'Activities associated with natural preferences are usually described with pleasure or with an offhanded manner, taking them for granted' (Myers *et al.*, 1998 p. 251).

Schein's (1993) 'career anchors' are similarly intended to help people find careers that fit fundamental aspects of their personalities. The anchors are a mix of values, needs, motives and abilities, and he emphasizes choosing just one anchor (Doyle, 2003 pp. 339–42). For example, people with a dominant service anchor may be best suited to careers like nursing and social work. Christine Doyle comments on an implication of this idea for career development. In one R&D team, it 'tended to consist of taking excellent programmers and promoting them to become untrained and inadequate managers who soon lost their technical edge' (2003, p. 341).

A current trend in career theory is towards a postmodern approach (Savickas, 1993; Bimrose *et al.*, 2003). Savickas (1993) suggested that career counselling's entry into the postmodern era is marked by six innovations. I think that these relate surprisingly well to MBTI theory. For example, one innovation is a rejection of the careers counsellor as expert, but rather as someone who creates 'a space where those involved can speak and act for themselves' (p. 211). The MBTI emphasis on clients deciding their own types, using MBTI results as indications and clues, is consistent with this. A second innovation is the replacement of the concept of 'fit' with 'enablement', and an affirmation of diversity. This is more arguable. MBTI theory sees both 'fit' and enablement as central.

Savickas further suggested a move towards 'grand narratives', 'life-design counselling', an integration of the career and the personal – a shift to an autobiographical approach and 'meaning-making'. These ideas seem to me consistent with the MBTI approach in their positive aspects, but rejecting a central and crucial idea in MBTI theory: that of *matching* stable aspects of personality and work. Fluidity and holism can be taken too far. Of the four levels of type interpretation and careers discussed by Jean Kummerow (1998) – static, dynamic, developmental and behavioural – the developmental level is the most relevant to postmodern approaches, and the static, 'snapshot' level to the next section.

Career choice

MBTI theory is quite a subtle approach to matching personality and careers. It recognizes that the *minority* types in a particular occupation can contribute to it in unusual and positive ways. Therefore it is far from just a 'pegs and holes' strategy, but it does raise questions to consider, e.g. 'Will I risk using my third and fourth functions too much?' and 'How will I explain my unorthodox approach to the job?'

Exercise 3.2

Step 1 Think of some times when you worked *very* effectively and particularly enjoyed it. What were you doing and did it reflect one or more of your preferences?

Step 2 Think of some times when you worked very *ineffectively*. What were you doing and did it reflect one or more of your non-preferences?

When doing this exercise you may like to use the job analysis checklist in the first section of Chapter 4. Possible complicating factors include stress (part of Chapter 7), type development (Chapter 2) and how sustained the kind of work was (Exercise 3.3).

Another subtle aspect of type theory is that it recognizes that many jobs can be done in a variety of equally effective ways. Scientists for example can be classifiers, explorers, artists, mystics, detectives, etc. Even a highly specialized occupation like chess grandmaster includes most of the types but – and this is crucial of course – they are said to differ in their characteristic styles of play (Kelly, 1985). Similarly, a major longitudinal study of doctors showed them both choosing and changing to specialisms typical of their types (McCaulley and Martin, 1995), e.g. ISFPs to anaesthetics from psychiatry, and INFPs the reverse.

Exercise 3.3

Step 1 Which elements of your current job (or a recent job) use your type's strengths? Roughly what proportion of your time are you or were you using your dominant function?

Step 2 Do you or did you want to use it more? If so, how?

Step 3 Which elements of your job use your fourth function? Roughly what proportion of your time? Is the proportion too much? ('Good for your character and hard on your nerves' is a positive interpretation of this situation) Or is it developmental?

Step 4 Do you want to use it less? If so, how?

For some people, their reaction to a job that makes little use of their dominant function, or too much use of their fourth function, is strong evidence for their psychological type.

Clear relationships between type and occupation have been consistently found in the US and other countries, and provide good evidence for the validity of the theory in general. Tables 3.1–3.6 illustrate these relationships. The tables near the end of Chapter 2 give the proportions of each type found in the general UK and US populations and some breakdowns of these provide comparison data. For example, a statement like 'ISTJs are often found in middle management' becomes more precise and meaningful when we can compare a figure from a representative sample of managers with the proportion of ISTJs in the general population.

Tables 3.1 and 3.2 show the MBTI types in good-sized samples of managers and administrators, and Tables 3.3 and 3.4 the MBTI types of fine artists and counsellors in the US. The proportion of each type in the two sets of tables is very different, from each other and from the general population. Tables 3.5 and 3.6 show US human resource workers and UK business psychologists.

The tables provide good evidence for MBTI theory. For example, the theory predicts that TJs will be drawn to administrative roles more than FPs are. Tables 3.1–3.6 show the following (percentages):

	TJs	FPs
Managers, etc.	54	11
School administrators	51	10
Fine artists	19	37
Counsellors	16	48
Human Resource workers	42	21
Business psychologists	29	32

Table 3.1 **MBTI types (%s) of US managers, administrators and supervisors (N = 4808)**

ISTJ	ISFJ	INFJ	INTJ
19	5	3	8
ISTP	ISFP	INFP	INTP
4	2	3	6
ESTP	ESFP	ENFP	ENTP
3	2	4	6
ESTJ	ESFJ	ENFJ	ENTJ
16	5	4	11

Source: Demarest (1997, p. 30)

Table 3.2 **MBTI Types (%s) of Canadian school administrators (N = 124)**

ISTJ	ISFJ	INFJ	INTJ
11	10	7	8
ISTP	ISFP	INFP	INTP
0	1	2	1
ESTP	ESFP	ENFP	ENTP
1	2	5	2
ESTJ	ESFJ	ENFJ	ENTJ
22	12	6	10

Source: Myers and McCaulley (1985, p. 39)

Table 3.3	**MBTI types (%s) of US professional fine artists (N = 114)**			
	ISTJ 2	ISFJ 3	INFJ 17	INTJ 7
	ISTP 0	ISFP 1	INFP 22	INTP 11
	ESTP 1	ESFP 0	ENFP 14	ENTP 0
	ESTJ 1	ESFJ 2	ENFJ 12	ENTJ 9

Table 3.4	**MBTI types (%s) of US practising counsellors (N = 359)**			
	ISTJ 6	ISFJ 6	INFJ 8	INTJ 3
	ISTP 1	ISFP 5	INFP 14	INTP 3
	ESTP 1	ESFP 6	ENFP 23	ENTP 3
	ESTJ 5	ESFJ 7	ENFJ 11	ENTJ 2

These are dramatic figures, though not the strongest differences either in these or similar Tables. For example, in Table 3.3, 91 per cent of the fine artists prefer N compared with 32 per cent of the general US population, while in a table not summarized here, 86 per cent of a sample of US independent studies students preferred FP (Myers and McCaulley, 1985 p. 42) compared with 28 per cent of the general population.

The human resource workers in Table 3.5 include more NFs than the administrative groups, and in this respect are more like the general US

Table 3.5	**MBTI types (%s) of US Human Resource workers (N = 380)**			
	ISTJ 10	ISFJ 4	INFJ 2	INTJ 9
	ISTP 2	ISFP 1	INFP 7	INTP 7
	ESTP 1	ESFP 3	ENFP 10	ENTP 9
	ESTJ 12	ESFJ 6	ENFJ 7	ENTJ 11

Source: Demarest (1997, p. 34)

Table 3.6	**MBTI types (%s) of UK business psychologists (N = 307)**			
	ISTJ 2	ISFJ 2	INFJ 4	INTJ 12
	ISTP 0	ISFP 0	INFP 14	INTP 10
	ESTP 0	ESFP 2	ENFP 16	ENTP 15
	ESTJ 5	ESFJ 3	ENFJ 6	ENTJ 10

population. Comparing the four types ST, SF, NT and NF in Tables 2.1, 2.2 and 3.1–3.6 gives the following figures:

	ST	SF	NF	NT
Gen. pop UK	36	41	14	10
Gen. pop US	37	33	16	17
Managers	43	14	31	14
School admin.	34	25	20	21
Fine artists	4	5	65	26
Counsellors	13	20	57	11
HR workers	25	13	26	36
Business psychologists	8	7	38	47

More generally, the relationships found between this variation of type and careers are:

ST	SF	NF	NT
Production	Teaching	Counselling	Science
Technical	Health care	Journalism	Architecture
Surgery	Sales	Arts	Engineering
Business	Service	Psychology	Design

The relationships are often substantial. Further examples: in the US, about 51 per cent of samples of artists and writers, 48 per cent of psychologists and 46 per cent of journalists are NFs, compared with about 16 per cent in the general US population. Conversely, only about 4 per cent of samples of farmers and about 4 per cent of the police are NFs (all these figures from Myers and McCaulley, 1985).

Myers believed the ST, SF, NT, NF types are the most relevant to career choice because they relate best to interests and motives central to work:

ST	–	'practical and matter of fact'
		Thus technical skills with facts and objects
SF	–	'sympathetic and friendly'
		Practical help and service to people
NT	–	'logical and ingenious'
		Theoretical and technical development
NF	–	'enthusiastic and insightful'
		Understanding and communication with people

(Myers and McCaulley, 1985; Lawrence, 1993)

Allen Hammer and Gerry Macdaid (1992) devised an ingenious test of this belief. They compared the percentage overlap of the top fifty careers of types that shared the functions (SN, TF) but had opposite attitudes (EI, JP), for example ISTJs and ESTPs, with types who shared the same attitudes but had opposite functions, e.g. ISTJs and INFJs. Types with the same functions but opposite attitudes averaged 41 per cent overlap, while those with the same attitudes but opposite functions averaged only 4 per cent overlap. Despite all the other influences on career choice, type has a clear effect.

Betsy Kendall's sample of 307 UK business psychologists (Table 3.6) shows that, compared with the UK general population (Table 2.1), they are overwhelmingly NP: 54 per cent compared with 15 per cent. What my simplified version of her data doesn't show is that all the (MBTI) types except ISTP were represented. (However, one of the presenters at the 2003 British Association for Psychological Type conference was an ISTP consultant and psychologist.)

In a further analysis of her data, Kendall compared employed and self-employed business psychologists and found a contrast between ENFPs and ENTJs:

	ENFP	ENTJ
Employed	5%	14%
Self-employed	19%	7%

Working for an organization seems to be more attractive to ENTJs than ENFPs. MBTI theory suggests the following possible motives: a greater desire to be unique individuals (ENFPs), and building and being a key player in a system (ENTJs) – among, of course, the many other factors affecting career choice.

Job satisfaction and job performance

In the last section I discussed some of the evidence that careers attract more of the types who, according to MBTI theory, will find the work most interesting. It seems obvious that they will also be satisfied with their work, and there is some evidence to support this. MBTI theory is more postmodernist here though, and correspondingly more difficult to test, because it takes a developmental and holistic view. Thus, the main idea is that each of us most enjoys work that requires us to use our dominant functions most and auxiliary functions second most. However, it also says that *some* use of third and fourth functions can also be enjoyable in a stretching way, helping type development, and that this will depend on how developed each preference is (as outlined towards the end of Chapter 2).

Another complication is that different types are likely to be satisfied and dissatisfied with different *aspects* of their work and for different reasons. Gill Clack's research on doctors is a good illustration. She found, in a large sample of 313 doctors, that Ts were significantly more satisfied with medicine as a career than Fs were, and suggested three possible explanations:

1 Ts are more able to cope with the highly competitive 'macho' culture of modern medicine, Fs need more harmony and appreciation than is currently the norm.

2 Ts are able to distance themselves more from their patients' suffering.

3 Ts and Fs have different definitions of 'job satisfaction' (Clack, submitted for publication).

Jean Kummerow (1998) further illustrated this new direction for research on type and career satisfaction in a qualitative study of librarians. She interviewed a librarian of each of the sixteen types about the aspects of their job that they particularly enjoyed. Each had found niches or specialisms, for example an ESTP included 'adapting technologies to the library's needs' and 'being away from her desk', an INFP 'Forming personal relationships with customers and enjoying their idiosyncrasies', and an INTJ 'Developing and working with policies and procedures and identifying the need for new ones' (p. 302).

Overall, although there is now quite a large literature on type and job satisfaction (Hammer, 1996; Kummerow, 1998) and a very large one on job satisfaction generally (Doyle, 2003), I think the main progress has been towards clarifying the most useful questions to ask and ways of asking them (too much reliance on rating scales) rather than producing solid findings. However, there is some useful support for MBTI theory, leading Hammer (1996) for example to conclude that 'those who are dissatisfied in an occupation tend to be those types who are opposite from the modal type in the occupation' (p. 40).

Obviously, motivation is central to job satisfaction and many other aspects of work. Ideas about the basic motives of each type and temperament were summarized in Chapter 2. Applying these ideas is first about *not* treating other people as like ourselves (unless they happen to be the same psychological type). The details of this application are discussed in Chapter 6 (communication), and Chapter 9 (leadership).

Of the two main management philosophies contrasted by McGregor (1960) – theory X and theory Y – MBTI theory is clearly in the theory Y approach, which sees people as naturally motivated to work for certain goals (MBTI theory is specific about these), given the right conditions (the theory is specific about these too). Box 3.2 on pp. 60–61 gives examples of key sources of motivation according to MBTI theory. In radical contrast, theory X sees people as intrinsically lazy, resistant to change, self-centred and unwilling to take responsibility.

Theory X probably seems obviously true to some people and Y to others, but I would say that neither is obviously true in the sense that we act on it. Will Hutton (2003), in a discussion of Richard Layard's ideas, argued that focusing on wanting to be happy as a motive 'turns the world on its head': 'Searching for happiness poses some uncomfortable and unsettling questions; the conventional economic and social wisdoms of the past 25 years are revealed as nonsense' (p. 30).

He is firmly in the theory Y approach, as the following examples show. Each is tested by Layard's question 'Does it make us happy?'

1 Unemployment. People generally don't seek it out or enjoy it. They search desperately for work.
2 Huge rewards for top executives. People don't work harder or better for extra pay when they're well-paid already. An extra pound for someone poor is worth far more to them than to someone rich.
3 Insecurity. People don't feel happier when they accept (or try to accept) job insecurity as part of an exciting enterprise culture.

Policies that follow from such considerations include less restructuring, more redistribution of income, and encouraging work environments. That way lies greater happiness. What MBTI theory adds to these general factors is specificity about the motives, and therefore kinds of activity, which are most fulfilling for each type.

If we take temperament theory for example, employees are more likely to be happy at work, and therefore to stay, if the following core needs are met through their work:

SPs   Acting according to the needs of the moment and having a speedy impact.
SJs   Belonging to a group and meeting responsibilities.
NTs   Becoming increasingly competent, and designing solutions to new problems.
NFs   Helping others to develop.

The theory says that if these needs are not met through work, then the results will be unhappiness and possibly leaving the job. This idea is consistent with research on realistic job previews (Premack and Wanous, 1985).

As an example of more specific ideas about sources of career satisfaction, let's take the most over-represented type (ENTJ) in US human resource workers and the equal most under-represented type

(ISFP). The following ideas are summarized and adapted from Paul Tieger and Barbara Barron-Tieger (2001, pp. 177, 348).

ENTJs	ISFPs
1 Leading, being in control, perfecting systems so they run efficiently	1 Consistency with inner values
2 Engaging in long-range strategic planning and creative problem solving	2 Attending to detail and working with real things that benefit other people
3 Well-organized environment where we work within clear and definite guidelines	3 Supportive and affirming environment
4 Working with complex and often difficult problems	4 Freedom to work independently but nearby other compatible and courteous people
5 Interacting with a variety of other capable, interesting and powerful people	5 Using my sense of aesthetics to enhance my physical work space
6 Opportunities to advance, and to increase and demonstrate my competence	6 Opportunities to experience inner growth in a quietly cheerful and co-operative setting

Thus some of the *strengths* of ENTJs are that they 'can be visionary leaders', 'work best in organizations where opportunities exist to rise to the top', and that they are 'ambitious and hard-working', 'good complex and creative problem-solvers' and 'able to keep long and short-term goals in mind'. Some of their *weaknesses* are that they 'may be demanding, critical and intimidating', 'may overlook relevant facts' and 'may not invite or permit input and contributions from others'.

In contrast, some of the *strengths* of ISFPs are their 'hands-on participation', that they 'welcome change and adapt well to new situations', are loyal and 'thrive in supportive and affirming climates'. Some of their *weaknesses* are that they 'may accept others' behaviour without seeking underlying meaning or motives', 'tend to take criticism and negative feedback personally', 'don't like to prepare in advance' and 'feel restricted by . . . bureaucracy'.

Tieger and Barron-Tieger (2001) suggest sources of job/career satisfaction for each of the 16 types, illustrating how fundamentally different they are, and, by implication, a direction for future research (Box 3.2).

Box 3.2	**Motives for career satisfaction (Tieger and Barron-Tieger 2001)**

ISTJs and **ISFJs** spend so much of their time reflecting on the realistic facts and details they personally experience, they derive the most satisfaction from performing work which allows them to use that data in a practical and useful way. (pp. 78–9)

In order for **ESTPs** and **ESFPs** to be happy, they must constantly be using their senses to experience the world. They like to be active, and they also like to be able to talk about and act on their observations. In general, the *process* is more important to them than the end result. ESTPs and ESFPs gain satisfaction just from the act of doing whatever it is they enjoy. (p. 79)

Both **INTJs** and **INFJs** must have work that makes use of their gift for seeing inner meanings, implications, and possibilities. They also like to get things done. It's important to them to find a way of expressing their perceptions. Somehow their unique, inner vision of how things could be must be translated into reality. (p. 80)

Because **ENTPs** and **ENFPs** love possibilities, they need to be free to pursue as many options as they can. To be satisfied, they also need to express their ideas or somehow make them real (for example, through a song, speech, or presentation). (p. 80)

Both **ISFPs** and **INFPs** need to feel good about what they do. They please themselves first and others second. Although their work often has to do with helping others, it must first and foremost be something they believe in wholeheartedly. (p. 81)

Both **ESFJs** and **ENFJs** derive their greatest satisfaction from pleasing others and receiving their approval. It is especially important for extraverted Feeling types to work in a harmonious environment that is free from interpersonal tension. (p. 82) ▶

Because they want to understand and make sense of the world, **ISTPs** and **INTPs** need work which allows them to make analyses – whether they are considering an abstract idea or a concrete project – in the most logical way possible. (p. 82)

Extraverted Thinking types need to be in charge. Both **ESTJs** and **ENTJs** need to be able to make logical decisions about the people and situations they encounter. Not content to merely observe the logic of things, they are happiest when they can use their skills to organize others to behave in the most logical and efficient way. (p. 83)

Good measures of job performance have also proved elusive, yet we can't really evaluate the effectiveness of selection procedures or training, or the assumed relationship with job satisfaction, without them. Even objective measures like sales figures can be affected by factors which are irrelevant to the particular salesperson, and difficult to take into account. Ratings by supervisors – the most widely-used method – are very open to bias. And an increasing amount of work is difficult to assess in terms of either process or outcome (Herriot and Pemberton, 1995)

Searching for a fulfilling career

Finding a fulfilling career often involves selling yourself, which is a very unattractive idea for some types. MBTI theory can help, first by explaining any distaste, second through using the descriptions to communicate your strengths. A specific, positive and accurate awareness of strengths can be useful for completing application forms, CVs and covering letters, in selection exercises, and in interviews. (I use the type descriptions in Hirsh and Kummerow 2000 as prompts for writing references too.)

Each type's strengths and weaknesses are also relevant to other aspects of searching for a fulfilling career. For example, at the level of developed preferences, Es are likely to be energetic, Is thorough, Ss realistic, Ns imaginative, Ts analytic, Fs warm, Js organized and Ps adaptable. These characteristics are firmly based in MBTI theory and therefore quite well supported empirically (Chapter 1).

The same applies to likely problems, e.g. Es may focus too broadly and Is too narrowly; Ss may neglect the medium and long term, and miss unusual job opportunities, Ns may have unrealistic expectations and miss important details; Ts may neglect values and Fs analysis, as well as be more sensitive to rejection; Js may decide too quickly and Ps not follow through.

Exercise 3.4

Step 1   Considering all aspects of searching for a career, which are you best at? And which are you worst at?

Step 2   Do your dominant and fourth functions explain these differences? Do the differences imply anything about your true type?

MBTI theory is thus relevant to the *process* of matching. It doesn't just say that there are these differences in people and related differences in jobs and that they should somehow fit together. Tieger and Barron-Tieger (2001) take a sophisticated and differentiated approach to each type in turn. For example, take INTPs (because the opposite type, ESFJ, is already fairly well-provided for in the standard career search literature). Tieger and Barron-Tieger (2001, pp. 227–231) suggest that INTPs' most effective strategies will build on their abilities to:

1 See possibilities that don't exist at the present time.
2 Create their own jobs.
3 Anticipate the logical consequences of action.
4 Create and implement an innovative job search.
5 Keep all their career options open to gather all the relevant and important information.

They also suggest possible pitfalls and, because they are generalizations and because of type development, further suggest that each INTP considers 'Is this true for me?' and 'How did this tendency prevent me from getting something that I wanted?' Thus these are *potential* pitfalls for INTPs:

1 Make sure to eventually move your plans out of the conceptual stage and into practice.

2 Establish realistic objectives and goals based upon what is practical, not on what your confidence tells you is possible.

3 Make sure you don't appear condescending or arrogant to potential employers.

4 Remember to follow through on important details.

5 Don't put off making a decision.

Like their advice generally, this seems to me highly pertinent. They also give good examples. The advice is very consistent with MBTI theory, but integrates their extensive experience too, and it would be valuable to test all their ideas formally and probably refine and add to them. For example, I think a good tone for Ps generally is to say 'Try a few things, see what happens' and 'Plans are calming for some people, others want to keep their options open.'

Other elements in searching for a fulfilling career are job advertisements, application forms and selection interviews. These are discussed in the next chapter.

Conclusions

MBTI theory is a flexible matching approach to careers which integrates traditional and postmodern elements. There are strong relationships between type and choice of career but the theory recognizes that minority types in a particular career can contribute to it in unusual and positive ways. They can also find and create niches, so studies of job satisfaction need to focus on different aspects of work and different motives. Similarly, the theory is very specific about strategies and potential pitfalls for each type in the process of searching for a fulfilling career.

4 Selection

MBTI theory can contribute to making many elements of selection more effective and ethical: job and person descriptions, advertisements, information sent to potential applicants, application forms, selection techniques and rejection letters. In this chapter, three of the elements are discussed in detail – job description, design of application forms and interviewing, especially interviewer training. Then I focus on three issues: (1) the tendency for selectors to choose people like themselves; (2) the relationship between Conscientiousness, the Big Five parallel to Judging/Perceiving, and job performance; and (3) use of the MBTI questionnaire in selection.

Job description

Are most selectors clear about what they want in a new employee? Job descriptions (what the person is expected to do) and person specifications (the characteristics a person needs to do a job well) are the standard strategies, but there are numerous methods for applying them, e.g. critical incidents technique and the rep grid (Doyle, 2003).

It has been argued that job descriptions are out of date because so many jobs now are short term or changing as a result of new technology, etc. A different problem is expecting too much; Christine Doyle cites a 1997 study of what employers want from their graduate employees and comments that it 'reads like a "wish list" for superhumans' (p. 271). However, although jobs aren't as stable as they were a few years ago, and some employers have unrealistic expectations, matching people and jobs still matters, as discussed in Chapter 3.

MBTI theory can be used to describe jobs. Many jobs require use of all a person's preferences and non-preferences but, crucially, to varying degrees. The central questions are: which preferences are called upon most to do the work? And then: which characteristics are *necessary* and which are *desirable*? The application of MBTI theory described next is relatively superficial, but practical. A sophisticated version would use expert judges, scoring weights and correlations with job performance. However, I say 'practical' because many selection systems actually used are a long way from the sophisticated ideal, but would be improved by greater clarity about the job.

I've based the MBTI Job Description below on the MBTI Step II level of the theory, e.g. Quenk *et al.* (2001) and Quenk (2003) and on Big Five descriptions, e.g. the NEO Job Profiler (Costa *et al.*, 1995) because they are more behavioural and specific than the basic (in the sense of fundamental) MBTI Step I, which measures the preferences. A quicker, but vaguer, variation would be to describe jobs in terms of the preferences themselves. The preliminary attempt below focuses on tasks and general skills, which is appropriate for contemporary, less stable jobs (Robertson and Smith, 2001).

Exercise 4.1   The MBTI Job Description

Step 1   Write the job title here:

Step 2   Rate each of the following characteristics on its degree of relevance to this job:

Characteristic	Highly relevant			Fairly relevant			Not at all	
	7	6	5	4	3	2	1	0

Confidence
Speaking and listening
Reading and writing
Lively, energetic
Working alone

Attention to detail
Original thinking ▶

Applying ideas
Openness to ideas

Analytic
Empathic
Tough-minded
Sympathetic

Organized
Flexible
Routine
Responsive to the unexpected

Step 3   Take each characteristic rated 7, 6 or 5 and categorize it as
Essential or Desirable.
It is usually practical to try to measure only four or five
characteristics.

Step 4   Consider how to measure each Essential characteristic.

MBTI theory emphasizes the most appealing as well as the most
distasteful duties. It also suggests that many of the characteristics in
the MBTI Job Description will tend not to be equally well-
developed in the same person, e.g. empathy (F) and tough-
mindedness (T). However, selection is concerned with type
development much more than with type itself.

Step 5   Consider how to measure each Desirable characteristic.

Two further sets of refinements would either enrich or overcomplicate
the MBTI Job Description. First, Chris Lewis's (1992) analysis of
recruitment and selection included a Job Analysis checklist (p. 110),
which, like Robertson and Smith's (2001) discussion of task and
worker-orientated kinds of job analysis, indicates the other stages and
aspects involved, and some subtleties not included in the MBTI Job
Description. It is:

1 Job title
2 Job context
3 Main duties

4 Most difficult duties

5 Most distasteful duties

6 Features of the work

7 Features of the workplace

8 Criteria used in evaluating performance

Moreover, characteristics associated with Anxiety are missing from the MBTI Job Description, and will often be relevant, e.g. 'Resilient' and 'Composed'.

Designing application forms

A central question in designing an application form (and in other elements of selection) is: is there any bias for or against a type or types? It is likely that a particular application form will appeal more to some types than others and that these early impressions will have their usual disproportionate power. Some organizations will be rejected because their brochures and forms are less attractive and the people rejecting them may be exactly the sort of people the organization wishes to recruit.

Exercise 4.2

Step 1   Can you think of application forms and other preliminary information that you've found boring, unappealing or worse? What was it about them (and you)?

Step 2   Any application forms or information that you were stimulated and attracted by?

Step 3   Does MBTI theory explain any of your reactions?

Step 4   Any implications for change?

Thus, Hai *et al.* (1986) related psychological type to four different styles of application form. They found that job applicants preferred those forms which were congruent with their own types. Participants were also asked to rank order the companies they would choose to work for; they preferred those which seemed most like themselves.

Debbie Fleck and myself (Fleck and Bayne, 1990) investigated type and judgements of a standard application form. The application form asked for personal details, education, employment, referees, with a third of a page for other relevant experience and two thirds of a page for other relevant information 'especially about your particular interests and why you wish to come to this organization.' Participants (thirteen STs, seven SFs, nine NFs and ten NTs) answered a nine-item questionnaire about the application form.

There were no differences between the answers of STs, SFs, NTs, and NFs to questions on formality, length, numbers of open questions, space available for personal comment, questions they would have preferred not to answer and overall 'satisfaction' with the form. (Questions 1–5 and 7). Question 6 asked whether there were any questions which they would like to have been asked. Seven out of nine NFs, but only two out of thirteen STs answered yes. The NFs wanted to be asked about hobbies, interests and personal feelings about why they thought they would get the job. In contrast the two STs would both liked to have been asked 'the minimum salary that I would expect'. Generally, SFs (five out of seven) and NTs (ten out of ten) did *not* want other questions.

Question 8 asked if they thought the form allowed them to do themselves justice. Six out of nine NFs thought not, compared with four of thirteen STs, three of seven SFs and one of ten NTs. The NFs wanted to express their individuality more with greater scope for personal comment while the STs wanted more space for qualifications and responsibilities. This pattern was consistent with responses to Question 6.

Question 9 asked participants how they would alter the application form. Seven of the thirteen STs said that they would not alter the form. Four wanted more specific questions to be asked and more space allowed for details. Two thought that it would be better to include a few more personal questions.

In Fleck and Bayne's study only two of the seven SFs said they would not alter the form. Two said that they would include more open-ended questions but would not have left so much space in which to answer them. The remaining three said they would include some more personal questions.

Only one of the nine NFs said she would not alter the form. Three would have included more open-ended questions, and another four wanted more emphasis to be put on personal experiences. The other said he would ask more personal questions.

Only two of the ten NTs said they would not alter the form. Three said they would make some technical changes such as changing the colour of the form (from yellow to white), putting the guidance notes on the front page instead of the last page, and making the boxes on the front page wider to allow for large writing. Two said they disliked the reference section, especially the fact that they were specifically asked for a reference from their first employer, and that it might not necessarily reflect on their abilities or do them justice. One said she would make the education section less formal and would include space for the applicant to explain educational choices made. Two said they would have preferred fewer open-ended questions.

One implication of these findings is that NFs may be deterred by standard forms, other things being equal. They may fill the forms in with less care or skill than people of other types, or fill in another organization's form instead. The general point is that application forms can be made more congruent with a particular psychological type, and thus gather better information and provide better public relations. They might also tend to deter applicants of some types, thus reducing in a useful way the number of applications to deal with. That may not be such good PR, but generally design of application forms seems worth more attention, particularly as they are an early cue for candidates to use in forming an impression of an organization.

Exercise 4.3

Step 1   Show an application form to people of different types to your own (preferably with different dominant functions), and ask for their reactions.

Step 2   Any implications for change?

Job advertisements come even earlier in selection than application forms, and are of course seen by far more people. The only research I know of related to type and advertisements is Matthews and Redman (1998). They found that the adjectives that were most likely to *discourage* applications from managers included 'analytical', 'creative' and 'energetic', which is interesting and puzzling.

> **Exercise 4.4**
>
> Analyse job advertisements from an MBTI perspective. What do they 'say' about the organization? Which types or temperaments might they appeal to? Do they seem to be the types most likely (as a general tendency) to fit the job?

A new aspect of application forms is the impact of putting them online. So far, the benefits appear to be for organizations rather than applicants. Ruth Price and Fiona Patterson (2003) interviewed twenty students who were also applicants and found that 85 per cent of them were concerned about lack of privacy (often forms are completed in a shared computer room) and 95 per cent felt dehumanized and that the process was 'unreal'. These were very clear findings which don't leave room for type differences. However, type does seem likely to affect *degree* of response. Price and Patterson propose several thoughtful, practical guidelines for improving online application forms, but their general conclusion from an exploratory study is that the forms may 'save money in the short-term due to the reduced cost of the hiring method, but in the long-term may lose ... reputation, quality employees and money' (p. 17).

Interviewing

The 'good interviewer'

The idea of a 'good interviewer' implies someone who is able to communicate well with a wide range of interviewees, gather relevant information from them, make accurate judgements about them and leave them feeling fairly treated. MBTI theory takes a more sober view. It suggests that each type will tend to be most comfortable with some interviewing skills and less comfortable with others.

Interviewer training

I think the main contribution of MBTI theory to giving feedback to trainee interviewers is twofold. First, it encourages constructive self-assessment. Trainees are often too harsh on themselves. Second, it provides a framework within which observers and trainees are helped to be specific and balanced, rather than bland and general or too critical. It is also a useful counter to myths about *the* way to interview.

Table 4.1 illustrates the likely interviewing strengths associated with each preference, and the likely weaknesses or areas to work on. The main general principle in an MBTI perspective on interviewer training is to develop or confirm the strengths of each trainee first and most, and then encourage them to add the strengths associated with the opposite type, but to a lesser extent. For example, MBTI theory predicts that interviewers with a preference for, and good development of, S will: (a) tend to observe non-verbal communications (NVCs) particularly well, but (b) tend to overlook themes or the general picture. According to MBTI theory, they should continue to observe NVCs well, and occasionally remind themselves that themes matter too.

Using Table 4.1 for giving feedback to oneself is possible, but can be more difficult than use in a group. It is too easy to assess oneself as skilful at observing NVC for example, when the judgement is a comparative one. I used to think I observed NVC well until I compared myself with two people with a well-developed preference for S.

One way of countering this tendency to inaccurate self-assessment is to use another principle from MBTI theory, that of *relative* development of opposing preferences. For example, if I compare my S and N interviewing skills (in Table 4.1), it's easy to say that my N skills are more developed. But still the benefits of working with a group of varied types and therefore being able to compare oneself directly with others of different types seem clear.

Exercise 4.5

Apply Table 4.1 to yourself as an interviewer, by self-assessment and by asking others for their views.

Preparing for selection interviews can be helpful to candidates as well as to their interviewers. They can identify incidents which illustrate relevant competencies, and then they practice talking about those incidents in ways that provide the kinds of information of most interest to interviewers who prefer Sensing, Intuition, etc. Table 4.2 lists some further suggestions for candidates.

Table 4.1	The preferences and aspects of selection interviewing	
	Likely strengths	Likely aspects to work on
E –	Easy initial contact Thinking 'on feet' Showing interest and enthusiasm	Paraphrasing more Using silence Helping the interviewee talk about issues in sufficient depth
I –	Asking the interviewee about a few issues in depth Using silence	Paraphrasing more Expressiveness Ease of initial contact
S –	Observing details Asking for details Being realistic	Taking the overall picture into account Using hunches
N –	Seeing the overall picture Seeing patterns, themes Using hunches	Being specific Asking for details Testing hunches Not showing impatience with details
T –	Being objective Challenging Being concise	'Picking up' emotions and feelings Being empathic Being warmer/less impersonal
F –	Being warm Being empathic Awareness of values	Taking thoughts into account as well as emotions and feelings Coping with conflict Being more objective
J –	Being organized Being decisive Planning the interview	Premature closure Being flexible
P –	Being spontaneous Being flexible	Being organized, e.g. keeping to time, structure of session Keeping focused

Source: Simplified and developed from Heinrich and Pfeiffer (1989)

In terms of interviewer skills, the four functions (S, N, T, and F) can all be related to different kinds of question, as in Table 4.3. The idea here is that each kind of question can contribute to an effective interview when asked skilfully, but that interviewers tend to overuse those kinds of question associated with their preferences.

In the structured interviews currently recommended (McDaniel *et al.* 1994; Taylor and Small 2002, 2003), though perhaps not widely adopted, the questions in Table 4.3 would be used as follow-ups to

Table 4.2	**The preferences and interviewee preparation**	
	Likely strengths	Consider preparing/practising
E –	Relating to the interviewer Talking easily	A strategy for being concise
I –	Comfortable with silence	Fuller answers
S –	Concrete examples	General points, themes
N –	Big picture Associations	Details Relevance
T –	Logic Conciseness	More warmth Empathy (with other people in incidents)
F –	Values Empathy	Logic Objectivity
J –	Preparation	A cautious element in opinions
P –	Flexibility Spontaneity	Relevance

Table 4.3	**The functions and kinds of question (examples)**	
Sensing	–	How often? When? For example? Where?
Intuition	–	Tell me about? Do any other possibilities come to mind? What if …?
Thinking	–	Why? Any other reasons? What about the case against?
Feeling	–	You sound particularly interested in that? What was going on for the other person?

questions about past experience. The different kinds of follow-up should add to the validity of descriptively anchored rating scales for each main interview question, though it is probably only large organizations which can afford to develop them. They can also be used to enrich semi-structured and unstructured interviews. Resent research (e.g. Blackman and Funder, 2002) suggests that unstructured interviews may be of high value when the aim, as it often is, is to accurately assess personality, both positive and what Blackman and Funder call 'counterproductive' traits.

Similarly, when the interviewer or panel are making decisions, MBTI theory suggests that the best decisions use both T and F (discussed in Chapter 9). This is in addition to allowing for biases for and against applicants because of their types as well, of course, as their gender, ethnicity, etc. For example, an interviewer who prefers Sensing might be impatient with and biased against an applicant who doesn't, as the interviewer sees it, 'stick to the point' or show realism, despite a person description which emphasizes original thinking. This application of MBTI theory raises the issue of cloning in organizations.

Three issues

Cloning

Cloning is the tendency, on the part of selectors, to choose people who are like them, in this case of similar temperament or type. This 'like me' bias can also play a part in promotion and other work decisions. It has been called the 'comfortable clone syndrome' by Leonard and Straus (1997 p. 112), but a more neutral and general term is 'Person–Organization fit' (Thomas and Anderson, 2002).

A match in important values and goals between workers and their organization is associated with higher job satisfaction, lower turnover and lower stress (Schneider 1987, 1997). A match in salient personality characteristics also contributes but is probably more problematic. In particular, it can contribute to difficulty in adapting. For example, Kroeger and Thuesen (1988, pp. 85–6) described a practice of six dentists who were all the same psychological type. They were very skilful, dedicated and efficient but their business was failing. They worked harder, but even fewer people came. Eventually, after consultation with Kroeger and Thuesen, they worked out that they needed other skills, in this case those associated with Extraverted Feeling and Intuition. They were then faced with a choice between developing these skills more themselves or recruiting staff who had them already. One of them started going to meetings, speaking at PTAs, etc., and the others agreed that this was as much a part of their work as filling teeth.

From an MBTI perspective this small organization had taken a long time to appreciate that their strengths had corresponding weaknesses, and that cloning of personality can be a liability. One preventive strategy is to conduct regular reviews of personality (and values) profiles, looking for the optimum Person–Organization fit for the organization (Schneider *et al.*, 1997; Thomas and Anderson, 2002). The organization's 'image' and selection and induction procedures play a part in maintaining that optimum fit. MBTI theory helps in deciding when cloning of personality is appropriate and valuable and when it's a bias.

Exercise 4.6

Does your organization have a 'type'? Try applying the preferences to your organization or department. Focus on 'how things work round here'.

Bridges (1992) finds organizational type an 'extraordinarily useful idea' and has designed a questionnaire, 'The Organizational Character Index', to apply it. For example, a TF item is 'Which better describes the leader's style – criticism or encouragement?' However, it may be most useful at the level of department or team, or to clashes between organization, departments and teams.

Which comes first – the people or the organization? Is it the kinds of people in an organization who have most effect on how it looks, feels and 'behaves', or does the organizational structure, etc. matter more? This question parallels the personality versus situation issue, or pseudo-issue, that troubled and dominated the psychology of personality for many years. From an MBTI perspective, the answer is that different kinds of organization attract and select different kinds of people, who then choose whether to stay or move on. The basic idea here is that the 'fit' between person and organization, or unit, matters, in the same way as the fit with the job itself does (Kristof, 1996). An implication is that organizations, like people, are hard to change in any fundamental way.

Step 1   Describe your ideal organization.

Step 2   Does MBTI theory relate to any aspect of your description?

This exercise usually works well with temperament groups (if possible) or SFs, TFs, NFs and NTs. The ideal organizations for each type are usually radically different and very revealing: ST groups tend to emphasize hierarchy, control and specific realistic goals with everyone knowing exactly what their job is; SFs a warm, personal atmosphere; NFs harmony, contributing socially and flexibility; and NTs efficiency, innovation and focus on global issues (Mitroff and Kilmann, 1975).

Conscientiousness (JP) and job performance

MBTI theory predicts choice of occupation, style of working and job satisfaction better than it does job performance. However, Myers with Myers (1980) did also suggest that the most competent workers would be doing jobs that are consistent with their type, so *some* relationship with job performance is expected. One of the problems for research on these predictions is the number of factors involved at both individual and organization levels, e.g. type development and how hierarchical the organization is.

The personality characteristic that so far correlates most strongly with job performance is Conscientiousness, the Big Five parallel to Judging versus Perceiving. The relationship is about .2 (Barrick and Mount, 1991; Salgado, 1997), large enough to be useful. From an MBTI perspective, the most interesting (and disturbing) aspect of this relationship is how over-interpreted it is, though this flaw does make more sense in Big Five terminology. For example, Mount and Barrick (1998) remark that

> Individuals who are dependable, persistent, goal-directed and organized tend to be high performers on virtually any job; viewed negatively, those who are careless, irresponsible, low achievement striving and impulsive tend to be low performers on virtually any job.

(p. 851)

'Careless' is part of the Big Five description of low Conscientiousness, or, in MBTI terms, a preference for Perceiving. From an MBTI perspective, relating P and carelessness (and poor job performance) is a serious error. First, .2 is a low correlation (although it can be defended as meaningful because of the large number of factors involved). Second, it may well conceal opposing relationships, i.e. P associated with good job performance in some circumstances and J with poor performance in others. MBTI theory predicts this very clearly; the strengths of Ps are vital in some jobs, as discussed in Chapter 3.

However, there are some signs, though rather grudging, in the mainstream literature, that some researchers are beginning to appreciate this. They do not, so far, include Mount and Barrick (1998) who equate Conscientiousness with general intelligence as a valuable predictor of good performance (p. 856). In contrast, Robertson *et al.* (2000) state that being unconventional and flexible is useful in some work situations and that high Conscientiousness 'may also serve to undermine certain aspects of managerial performance' (p. 173). However, this more balanced and accurate view, from an MBTI perspective, is not yet apparent in the literature generally (e.g. Judge *et al.*, 1999).

Should the MBTI questionnaire be used in selection?

The questionnaire was not designed to measure ability, or development of type, and at best does not measure them well, so if it is used in selection it should be as one of a sophisticated set of procedures, and mainly to suggest hypotheses and to be one piece of evidence among many. The issue is partly an empirical one and partly wider. Empirically, Big Five measures are related to work performance. MBTI results correlate highly with Big Five results, therefore the MBTI questionnaire too can be used in this way. Faking does not seem in practice to be a problem (Bayne, 2004) and in any case is more likely to be detected through other elements of a selection procedure. The wider issue is that if the MBTI questionnaire is used (and especially misused) for selection this will probably detract from its intended purposes of personal and professional development. On the other hand, if selection procedures generally have become more two-way, which seems to be the case (Anderson and Cunningham, 2000), then MBTI results with skilled feedback could play a central and very positive role.

Using the MBTI questionnaire in selection may clash with APT's Ethical Principles. The first two principles are that completing the questionnaire should be voluntary and that the results should only be given to other people with informed consent. Are applicants for a job volunteers? And does knowledge of the procedures amount to informed consent? In other words, are applicants coerced because they want the job?

Conclusions

Matching people and jobs is still important, despite more jobs being short-term and changing more quickly. MBTI theory gives valuable perspectives on job descriptions, application forms, selection interviewing and interviewer training. Applying the theory can, for example, reduce cloning and enhance both accuracy of judgement and public relations. Further, the theory strongly suggests that research relating Conscientiousness to job performance discriminates unfairly against Ps.

5 Time

Psychological type has a deep influence on attitudes towards time, which is reflected in expressions like 'So little time, so much to do', 'Such a waste of time', 'time famine', and 'Never put off until tomorrow what you can do the day after tomorrow.' Actually, it's the tone of the first of these that matters most. If said impatiently, wearily or purposefully, it has a J flavour, but said calmly or ironically, it's more P. I see the next two as J in their conception of time and the last one as P.

Exercise 5.1

How do you react to each of the expressions about time in the first paragraph? Do you have any favourite metaphors for time, or phrases about it?

Exercise 5.2

Step 1 If you've been on a time management course, what effect did it have on you? Have you continued to use any of the techniques?

Step 2 Did any of the techniques not work for you?

Step 3 Does MBTI theory help to explain your reactions to the techniques?

Courses on time management are popular, and effective for some people. From an MBTI perspective, they're usually heavily biased towards a J approach (and possibly SJ) and thus tend to leave Ps unchanged, or defeated and demoralized by their failure to benefit, when it's the approach which is at fault. Moreover, time management courses may also affect some people with a preference for J badly, by encouraging them to be *too* time-conscious or *too* organized.

The general perspective on time from MBTI theory is of course that different approaches suit different types and that if the differences are not respected they can cause a lot of conflict. Further, JP seems to be the most important preference where time is concerned, but the other preferences play a part and so does whole type. In this chapter I discuss time and

1 The influence of JP.
2 The influence of the other preferences.
3 Related research and ideas on the types and time, procrastination, 'Introverted Complexity No. 47' and time perspective.

JP and time

The phrase 'time management' is strongly J. For Ps, time just happens, it flows; *managing* it doesn't feel at all right. This difference stems from basic motives and has wide implications. The basic motives are to control and organize (J) versus to adapt and be flexible (P). Thus, the starting position of Js is that free time is what's left over after planned activities, while for Ps, it's that time is free, except what's planned.

Potential problems with time for Js include premature closure, which may mean either poor-quality work or having to redo the work, and continuing to work on something that's become irrelevant just so that it's completed. Js may also feel driven and thus unable to relax. Some Js can be obsessive. Potential problems for Ps include feeling their natural approach is wrong (because that message is often given) and not completing on time, because some tasks – obviously, more complex ones – are too complex to do in the last few hours. They can also be 'adrenaline junkies'. Conversely, some Ps may feel too laid back and thus unable to motivate themselves.

The conflicts that can result between Js and Ps are obvious. For example, one person in a team works best at the last moment and another wants to start early. The first person thrives on an imminent deadline energy surge, the second works best by completing work well before a deadline. Can they find ways of working together successfully?

Kroeger with Thuesen (1992) make a subtle point here about a strategy that is counter-productive, but very tempting. One person makes an effort to help the other by behaving out of preference – for example a J has behaved more spontaneously and flexibly with a P colleague than they wanted to, and the P colleague says 'That was great. You can do it. Next time we work together will be easier still.' Or even, 'Why don't you relax and just let things happen more often?'

For balance, let's also take the opposite example. A P starts work on a project early. The danger is that their J colleague says: 'That was great. You can do it. Next time we work together will be easier still.' Or even 'Why don't you get the rest of your life organized too?'

In both examples, the speaker may mean well but is not respecting the other's different motives and style. A simple 'Thank you' would have been better, and would have appreciated the effort involved without trying to change the other person into their opposite.

The much more realistic approach is for Ps to add a little organization to their natural strengths, and for Js to add a little flexibility to theirs. People with each preference usually benefit from some qualities of the opposite preference, either in themselves through type development, or by acknowledging its value in a co-worker or manager, and allowing them to have some influence. For example, Ps can counter Js' tendency to be rigid and compulsive in their approach to time, and Js can counter Ps' tendency to return to work which is finished, or sufficiently so. There is a time to stop!

The optimistic view, which seems true to me but hasn't been investigated rigorously, is that this mild balancing effect happens naturally with age (through type development). MBTI theory's contribution is of course to make the constructive use of difference more likely and to speed it up in some cases. An alternative way of putting this is that people can learn skills specific to certain situations without changing their basic personality or feeling compromised or false.

From an MBTI perspective, therefore, the way forward starts from recognizing strengths in self and others, e.g. the task focus and organization of Js, the multi-tasking flexibility of Ps. This may mean both being clear about your way of working to others who are affected by it and sometimes modifying your own style a little, through negotiation. These general principles can be – need to be – adapted by each individual. For example, I think a strength of developed Ps is that they have a sense of timing that lets them know when to 'change gear'. However, this sense of timing does need to develop and become reliable and trusted; how Ps do this hasn't been studied yet.

A personal example which describes some aspects of it is that before writing this book I sketched a rough and very provisional plan, and worked out how long I had per chapter, or, rather, first draft of each chapter allowing lots of time for rewriting. This was a kind of mental trick, because my ideal way of writing would be in short bursts (an NP characteristic) followed by long periods in which, occasionally, I'd cross out a sentence, move a paragraph or replace a word. Eventually I'd give the manuscript to the publisher. By creating deadlines for each draft chapter, I was making use of the imminent deadline energy surge experienced by some Ps. Another mental trick I use is to remember one of my lecturers saying to me, rather wistfully, when I was a postgraduate student 'Publish your drafts'. This excellent advice combats perfectionism, and is also an example of task (rather than time) management, a strategy discussed in the section on 'Introverted complexity No. 47'.

The other preferences and time

EI

Exercise 5.3

Imagine that you've been given three free days. What would you most like to do?

Es tend to choose lots of activities, most of them sociable, while Is tend to choose a few activities, mostly solitary ones. Es tend to find Is' activities boring, Is tend to find Es' activities exhausting.

The implications for Es and use of time are for them to respect their strengths, which lie in action, including talking, and to build in, where useful and necessary, some introverted time and recognize that they can be distracted. The implications for Is are to respect their strengths, which lie in reflection, including privacy, and to build in, where useful and necessary, some time for discussion and action.

SN

The strengths of Ss in their use of time are to be realistic, aware of details and able to break tasks down into sequential steps. The strengths of Ns are their belief that all things are possible, their awareness of the 'big picture' and their openness to new ways of doing things, e.g. missing out some steps without loss of quality.

Ss and Ns can therefore benefit from consulting and respecting each other's approach and views. This can be very hard: one person's chaos is another's system, some people value details (lots of exact, precise details), others don't.

TF

The strengths of Ts in their use of time include task focus (and analysis) and efficiency, and they give these priority over 'people issues'. The main strength of Fs is their awareness of impacts on themselves and others – their capacity for empathy. Kummerow *et al.* (1997) suggest several tips for Ts and Fs, e.g. to people who work with Ts, that

> their task focus is natural and efficient for them. It's not necessarily that they are trying to avoid people issues. Ask for the time you need to process interpersonal issues; make clear the urgency of the issue, e.g. 'I can't contribute further until we talk about these things.'
>
> (p. 69)

Conversely, people who work with Fs can recognize that Fs' awareness of people's reactions can be crucial.

The general usefulness of Ts and Fs for each other is expressed well by Kroeger with Thuesen (1992):

> Ts used Fs to remind them that process is as important as product. In other words, if you get through the day but alienate people in the process, your bottom-line productivity is questionable. And Fs need Ts to keep them from getting too embroiled in daily interpersonal dynamics. Getting through the day means more than simply everyone getting along and liking you – you have to get something done.
>
> (p. 92)

Tips for SJs, NJs, SPs and NPs

In this section, I've selected what I think are the most useful ideas and tips for each of four combinations of preferences, from Fitzsimmons (1999), Kroeger and Thuesen (1988), Kummerow *et al.* (1997) and other sources. At a general level, they extend considerably the range of techniques usually recommended. At a personal level, the strategy is of course to consider trying those suggested for your own type first and see what works best for you, or, if you're happy with your current approach, to compare these tips with it.

SJs Timetables and calendars.
Lists which are specific, worked through systematically and checked off each day.

NJs Use lists as guides and to give an overview.
Natural planners (long- and short-term) who work in bursts.

SPs Work on whatever is needed at the time – what seems urgent and important.
Find ways to make things fun and efficient.

NPs Many projects at different stages, but no tight scheduling.
Ideally, life unfolds, with some help at the last minute from deadlines.
Work best from inspirations not plans.

In contrast, some of the rules advocated in standard time management course are heavily biased in favour of SJs and against NPs. For example:

A messy desk is the sign of a cluttered mind.

If you can find things and do your work, a 'messy' desk isn't a problem for you, yet some organizations impose cleared desks.

Don't put it down until you file it.

For some people, filing doesn't work. They need things where they can see them, hence a messy desk (which is actually organized into meaningful piles).

Finish one task before beginning another.

Some people work most creatively on several tasks at once, finding the changes refreshing.

Handle each piece of paper only once.

Sometimes it's too soon to respond to the piece of paper. You need more information or just more time to consider it, or it's a lower priority than other pieces of paper at the moment.

Fitzsimmons's study

The main study so far specifically on type and time was original and exploratory. Sharon Fitzsimmons (1999) asked five or more people of each type for their stories about occasions when they were successful in managing their time, the kinds of difficulties they have, and their suggestions for others of their type. Her approach thus assumes that successful people of the same type are the best source of realistic techniques for that type. She also circulated the stories to people of the same type for comment. Their reactions were generally very positive – to her astonishment in some cases!

The stories show themes consistent with MBTI theory and with this chapter but there are also variations (as is to be expected from a theory which categorizes, but recognizes individuality), and some participants reported ways of working which worked well enough for them, but did not feel as natural as they'd like. I recommend reading the stories for your own type and the types of close colleagues. You may well find a 'kindred spirit' and an effective suggestion.

Fitzsimmons included summaries for each type in five sections:

1 Expected characteristics
2 Driving force
3 Problem *most* likely to occur
4 Solutions *least* likely to be followed
5 Suggestions

My own attempts at sections 1 and 2 are in Chapter 2 of this book, and suggestions (section 5) were made earlier in this chapter. Examples of the characteristic problems and least likely solution found by Fitzsimmons, which generally seem clearly consistent with MBTI theory, are listed in Table 5.1. For a *more* likely solution for you, try the

| Table 5.1 | **Type, difficulties and *least* likely solutions** |
	Characteristic difficulties	Least likely solutions
ISTJ	Frustration with others' different work-styles. Overload.	Go with the flow.
ISFJ	Overload.	Do less.
INFJ	Conflict between wanting closure and helping others/achieving perfection.	Stop questioning and just do it.
INTJ	Frustration with interruptions and loss of interest in some projects.	Lower your standards.
ISTP	Being seen as not taking work seriously.	Follow a routine.
ISFP	Being distracted, forgetting, losing interest.	Make a careful plan and stick to it.
INFP	Being very tired (from trying to achieve perfection)	Use someone else's structure.
INTP	Losing interest.	Follow a routine.
ESTP	Relying too much on improvising.	Plan ahead.
ESFP	Being distracted.	Make a careful plan and stick to it.
ENFP	Being distracted.	Working steadily until the task is finished.
ENTP	Being distracted.	Ignore the new possibilities.
ESTJ	Frustration with unexpected obstacles.	Slow down.
ESFJ	Overload.	Work on your own. Shut yourself away.
ENFJ	Conflict between wanting closure and helping others.	Saying no (to everyone).
ENTJ	Overwork.	Do less.

Source: Modified from Fitzsimmons (1999)

least likely for the opposite type to your own, e.g. if your type is ISTJ, consider the ENFP unlikely solution.

The tips and ideas reviewed earlier in this chapter can be very useful, but it can also be worthwhile going deeper. Three possibilities are discussed in the rest of this section: Provost's (1998) suggestions about each type's reasons for procrastination; Kroeger's ideas about proper use of the dominant function; and Zimbardo's work on time perspective.

Procrastination

Procrastination is a severe problem, affecting about 50 per cent of the population (Dewitte and Lens, 2000). Judy Provost (1998), on the basis of many years experience with university students, suggested that people of all the types (definitely not just Ps) can procrastinate, but for different reasons. She suggested five main causes:

1 Perfectionism.
2 Task doesn't 'grab' the person.
3 The thrill of not finishing, of keeping it open.
4 Overstimulation – too many possibilities and ideas.
5 Avoiding tasks that stimulate feeling incompetent.

> ### Exercise 5.4
>
> You may like to identify or speculate about (a) which of these causes of procrastination is the most likely (or actual) threat to you, and (b) which psychological types are most likely to be affected by each of them.

Provost's experience with each of the causes is as follows. Perfectionism affects ISFJs, ISTJs and the four IN types most. INFPs and INTPs need to be 'grabbed' more than other types do. ENFPs and ENTPS are the most likely to resist closure and also to be overstimulated. Over-stimulation is also a major factor for INTJs and INFJs, but in them the overwhelming number of ideas comes more from within. Finally, it is ESTJs and ENTJs who find a feeling of incompetence particularly threatening (though temperament theory would suggest this cause as threatening to NTs too).

Obviously, it's sometimes crucial to identify underlying factors and choose interventions accordingly. Provost's (1998) approach to procrastination contrasts with the mainstream one (e.g. Dewitte and Lens, 2000), which – no surprise here – unfairly criticizes Ps and, oversimplifying a little, tries to turn them into Js.

'Introverted Complexity No. 47'

Another sophisticated application of MBTI theory in this area is Otto Kroeger's (undated) ideas about 'Introverted Complexity No. 47'. This tongue-in-cheek title reflects his ENFJ reaction to Is. I interpret his ideas here as in part task management rather than time management, but mainly as an example of the benefits of behaving like your own type.

By task management I mean focusing on the tasks you need or want to make progress with or complete in whatever length of time you choose and, either implicitly and intuitively or explicitly and literally, giving each task a proportion of that time. For example, lecturers tend to give too much time to one element of a very diverse set of tasks. That element is lecture preparation and, inevitably, there is less time for the other elements. Task management is giving a proportion of time to preparing lectures which takes into account the other tasks, by giving them each their share of time. Good task management thus deals with the problem of not enough time, unless of course your job asks you to do too many tasks, but that is a different problem.

Exercise 5.5

Step 1   Is there a task in your job that you give too much time to?

Step 2   The next step is obvious. Try giving less time to it (and therefore potentially more to other tasks). Alternatively, is it possible to cut or delegate one or more of your tasks?

MBTI theory's contribution to task management through Introverted Complexity No. 47 is as follows. It is directly relevant to Is, and indirectly relevant to Es who manage, coach or counsel Is.

In his article, Kroeger develops an implication of the idea in type dynamics that an introvert's dominant function is introverted. He argues that there is inevitably a conflict between the demands of the external world and the time and space needed by the dominant, and that an overactive auxiliary and a neglected dominant may be the result. Moreover, everyone, including the introvert themselves, may believe that the auxiliary is actually the dominant, which would be another kind of false type development. Kroeger suggests two sets of diagnostic questions to try to prevent or at least recognize a neglected dominant.

For IJs they are:

1 Do you find yourself pushed to finish what you start?
2 Do you have trouble setting yourself apart and relaxing?
3 Would you rather do a job yourself than trust it to someone else?
4 Would you rather schedule your private time rather than just let it happen?
5 Would you rather take charge of an event and move it towards completion?

For IPs, Kroeger suggests the following questions:

1 Do you find yourself following the moment?
2 Is your day more 'starts' than follow-throughs?
3 Is your life 'piles' of things to do someday?
4 Do you have trouble finding time for yourself?
5 Do your 'best laid plans often go astray'?

He suggests that three or more 'yes' answers to the appropriate set of questions is a good indication that Introverted Complexity No. 47 is gaining on you – probably in an insidious way – or it has a firm hold already. It is easy to believe that the outside world is more important but introverts believe this at their peril and should not be 'led astray' – dominated – by their auxiliaries. Therefore IPs benefit from focusing on and finishing things most of the time (IPs are Js in their inner world) and IJs benefit from being focused and relaxed and not worrying about finishing things and about schedules most of the time (IJs are Ps in their inner world).

Time perspective

Exercise 5.6

Step 1 Reflect for a moment on the future.

Step 2 How far – minutes, days, years, etc. – did you look ahead?

Step 3 Compare your results with the findings briefly discussed in this section.

Zimbardo argues that 'time perspective' is a very powerful influence on behaviour, and that a *balanced* time perspective increases effectiveness and fulfilment. He distinguishes five time perspectives: past-negative, past-positive, present-hedonistic, present-fatalistic and future (Zimbardo and Boyd, 1999). MBTI theory includes some related ideas. For example, Mann *et al.* (1968) speculated about dominant sensing types as follows:

> Those who live primarily in the present have little ability and less wish to anticipate or look ahead. It is from this lack of concern with the past or future, that is, an almost total reliance on the present, that the sensation type's primary personality traits derive.

> (p. 45)

It seems plausible that time perspective is a powerful influence on behaviour and experience.

In Zimbardo's model, a past-time perspective is associated with family and tradition; present-hedonistic with enjoying the present moment, as in the quote from Mann *et al.* (1968) above; present-fatalistic with hopelessness and powerlessness; and future with working for long-term goals. 'A future oriented individual lives in abstraction, suppressing the reality of the present for the imagined reality of an ideal future world' (Boniwell and Zimbardo, 2003, p. 129).

Both Zimbardo and MBTI theory see some degree of balance in time perspective as desirable, and both see people as capable of achieving it. The general practical implication is to move from advocating the same time management strategies for everyone to developing individualized strategies based on understanding workers' psychological types and how balanced their time perspective is. In addition, MBTI theory sees an emphasis on one of the time perspectives as natural for most of the types, and supplementing it, rather than equal facility with all of them, as desirable.

There are clear links between MBTI theory and Zimbardo's model, most obviously between SJ and past-positive; SP and present-hedonistic, and N and future. Harrison and Lawrence (1985) investigated how far people of each type looked into their futures. This was an important study for two reasons. The first is that it tested and strongly supported a central element of type dynamics. The second is the most relevant here: they predicted and found an almost perfect correlation between the sixteen types and time orientation. As they modestly remarked: 'Correlations of .97 are uncommon in psychological data' (p. 28).

The main finding was that the four dominant intuitive types looked furthest ahead, e.g. INTJs (N dominant) looked an average of thirty-three years ahead compared with the fifteen years of ENFJs (N secondary) and eight years of ISFPs. Bayne and Kwiatkowski (1998) replicated this main finding, with a lower but still very respectable correlation of .57, but considered that their measurement of time orientation could be much more thorough and accurate, and that there would then be a higher correlation.

Conclusions

Standard time management courses are usually biased towards people with a preference for J. The MBTI perspective is that different approaches to time suit different psychological types. The differences also explain some conflicts and clashes. MBTI theory offers solutions and strategies, an approach to managing procrastination, and some ideas about 'time perspective' as an underlying factor in our attitudes towards time, and therefore our effectiveness and sense of fulfilment. The main theme is to find your own ways of managing or living with time and not to impose ways on others.

6 Communication

Ideally, all conversations would end with each person having said what they wanted to, in the way they wanted, and with each person listened to and understood: there would be true contact, a 'meeting of minds', good communication. Psychological type is an important factor in good communications, but, as in career choice, does not explain everything. It does explain some misunderstandings, rejections and hostilities, or aspects of them, and suggest strategies. A basic assumption is that *all* types can communicate well with each other, though with characteristic difficulties.

Exercise 6.1

Step 1   Think of two conversations at work, one that went well, and one that was frustrating, and their effects on you, the other people and your organization.

Step 2   Does MBTI theory suggest any insights or strategies?

An example of the impact of knowing about EI on communication is that an E colleague now sees Is as 'needing time to reflect' rather than 'slow and boring', and she has made a corresponding change in her behaviour. Instead of bouncing into an I's office to discuss an issue, quite often being disappointed by the result, and being seen by the colleague as insensitive and rushed, she now – especially for complex issues – gives some warning. Their relationship has improved. Similarly, an NT who, consistent with MBTI theory, enjoys a good debate, now generally chooses to have them with other NTs and to be more sensitive to the different reactions to debates of people who are not NTs, e.g. their greater need to stop earlier (or not to start), and not to play devil's advocate.

MBTI theory suggests that effective communicators are, among other qualities and skills:

1 aware of their own main communication style(s);
2 aware of their likely impact on others of different styles;
3 able to adapt in order to improve communications and manage or resolve conflict.

In this chapter I discuss four communication 'languages', the associated potential clashes and strategies, and 'six contexts': writing; selling and influencing; giving and receiving feedback; assertiveness; teams and team-building; and training.

The emphasis in this chapter is firmly on verbal communication. However, non-verbal communication (NVC) plays a major part in communicating well. In effect, when talking to someone, two conversations are going on at once, verbal and nonverbal, giving human communication great richness. NVC allows us to be ironic but also makes misunderstandings more likely.

MBTI theory doesn't have much to say about NVC, except to suggest certain NVCs as clues to the preferences and temperaments (Bayne, 2004). An exception is Sondra VanSant's (2003) book on type and conflict. For example, she suggests that communication is helped by making slight adjustments towards the NVC of the other person. Thus, with EJs, sit and stand closer, have more direct eye contact, lean forward more, and use hand movements for emphasis; with EPs, make large gestures and move around more; with IJs, keep a physical barrier, break eye contact more and make 'understated' hand movements; and with IPs, have an informal stance, make eye contact less and move less (2003, pp. 50–1). VanSant emphasizes that these are all tendencies.

Such a strategy may sound bizarre but VanSant makes the useful analogy of learning a few phrases of another person's language (in the sense of French, Chinese, etc.), which is usually much appreciated. Changes in your NVC are of course usually less obvious but may also be appreciated and be quite natural. Brock takes the same approach to type differences in speech, which are discussed next.

Four 'languages'

The most influential approach to type and communication so far is Susan Brock's. She focused first on selling (Brock, 1994) and then on health care (Allen and Brock, 2000). In both settings, she found the most useful level of type theory to be the functional pairs: ST, SF, NF, NT. These pairs affect mainly the content and tone of communication while EI affects the pace and JP a tendency to move towards closure or to keeping things open.

An overview of the four 'languages' suggested by Brock is:

- ST language is brief and concise, emphasizes facts and logic, does not go off on tangents, and starts at the beginning.
- SF language has the same practical, sequential flavour as ST but is warmer, friendlier, and more personal.
- NF language is holistic, personal and general, and points to interesting possibilities with details to be 'worked out later'.
- NT language has the same general flavour as NF but emphasizes intellectual competence and reasoning more, is calm and objective.

All the types say that what they value is being listened to and honesty – but, crucially, interpret these qualities differently, as indicated in the languages.

The language most used in speech by each type is thought to reflect the characteristics of one of the function pairs (Brock) or the extraverted function (Thompson, 1998). There isn't enough evidence yet to decide which of these views is most useful (Bayne, 2004). If it's Dick Thompson's view, then Es use their dominant function most (ES, EN, ET or EF) and Is their auxiliary. For example, ISTJs and ESTJs both use T, INFPs and ENFPs both use N. More simply, there are four languages as follows:

SPs – S
NPs – N
TJs – T
FJs – F

Thompson sees these languages as having the relevant characteristics of the preferences, e.g. S being realistic, concrete, etc., and as fairly easy to observe accurately (Bayne, 2004).

Flexing

Brock argues that matching the other person's language, which she calls 'flexing', is easier than matching their type because, like Thompson, she considers that the languages are easier to observe. Moreover, a person's language may change quickly and you can then switch too. This can be done manipulatively but I think it's something many people do without thinking about it and without manipulative intentions. It's part of being empathic and sometimes (perhaps often) people adjust to each other in this natural way. Knowing about the four languages can make the process of matching more effective and easier.

Clashes

The general characteristics of the preferences which seem most relevant to communication styles and conflicts are:

Between E and I	Need to talk versus time to reflect
Between S and N	Details, being practical versus general picture, speculation
Between T and F	Objectivity versus values and impact on others
Between J and P	Push for closure versus keeping things open

Exercise 6.2

Think of negative words used to refer to each of the characteristics above, e.g. Es may see Is as secretive, boring and dull rather than 'taking time to reflect'. These perceptions can, of course, be serious obstacles to communication.

Some further examples of negative words for each preference are: pushy, intrusive, noisy (Is of Es); unrealistic, dangerous, mad (Ss of Ns); plodding, boring, nit-picking (Ns of Ss); soft, wet, illogical, too sensitive (Ts of Fs); cold, critical, unkind, unsympathetic (Fs of Ts); wishy-washy, aimless, frivolous (Js of Ps); control freaks, driven, inflexible (Ps of Js). I've tried to be even-handed here but the strength of meaning of the terms probably varies by type and for other reasons.

> ### Exercise 6.3
>
> Do you use any of the words in the previous paragraph, or similar ones, to describe aspects of any of the preferences? It's normal to do so, but the MBTI approach, of course, is to suggest noticing them and challenging them.

Some further examples of clashes between Js and Ps (modified from unpublished work by Valerie Stewart), are:

J: I'd like us to set some objectives.
P: What I do is my business and I'll do it my way.

J: I'm the boss.
P: That's your problem.

J: I didn't get where I am today without hard work and effort.
P: I didn't get where I am without enjoying myself.

P: This is not a battle we can win.
J: We'd better put more effort and resources in.

P: We don't have to decide yet.
J: We need a decision.

P: I'm not going to sell my soul for their idea of success.
J: There are rules.

Some people look at such examples and comment that they say all of them. They are misunderstanding the theory, which is about preferences: people do, on occasion, behave in ways which are not typical of them, but type focuses on what is typical, on tendencies and patterns, and most people are more likely to say one in each of the pairs of J and P comments than they are to say the other.

Strategies

MBTI theory tries, as discussed in Chapter 1, to be positive as its main emphasis, and the strategy of reframing is a logical consequence. For example, Ts can reframe Fs' 'softness' as a concern for people's morale and for harmony, and Fs can reframe Ts' 'detachment' as a concern for analysis and for improvement through criticism. Seeing differences constructively in this way can be difficult but is a practical possibility. It can also be taken further, treating the differences as constructive and even refreshing, e.g. that the calmness, generally, of Is can complement the energy, generally, of Es, and that Ps can benefit from Js' seriousness and Js from Ps' playfulness. The very qualities that can irritate and demoralize can also be stimulating and productive.

Other strategies for improving communication between you and someone of an opposite preference are discussed later in this section, but first you may like to try the following Exercise.

Exercise 6.4

Think of someone with a different preference or preferences to your own who you'd like to communicate better with. What change in your approach might MBTI theory suggest as worth trying? This might be quite a small change, as in the EI example earlier. The change definitely shouldn't mean you behaving like a different person. That would be a misuse of the theory.

The following general strategies for Es and Is follow directly from the theory:

Es to Is	Give Is time to reflect. Give Is time just to be alone – probably more time than you think.
Is to Es	Remember that Es tend to think out loud and to need contact – more contact than you think. Remember that Es, especially EPs, are trying out ideas and may sound as if they're making decisions when they're not.

Jonathon Rauch (2003) in his article 'Caring for your introvert' wrote that by discovering that he was an I after years of denying it, and coming out as an I, he had liberated himself from numerous damaging misconceptions. His first way of caring for himself is ensuring he has enough time alone. For him this means roughly two hours alone for every hour of socializing. He comments that this isn't antisocial or a sign of depression. It's as necessary as sleeping or eating. I think this is fair, but that he goes too far when he adds that Es wilt when alone and that they can't imagine why someone would need to be alone. Clearly, he's suffered for many years, but many Es need time alone too, and understand that people vary.

What's your reaction to Rauch's formula of two hours alone for every one socializing? How does it fit with your preference for E or I (or neither)? Do you have a formula of this kind?

We don't know yet how typical of Is Rauch's formula is. We do need a complementary article on caring for your extravert.

Rauch ends his article with a cry from the heart about caring for the introvert in your life. First, he wants everyone to recognize that being introvert isn't a choice. Second, he'd like you, when you see an introvert lost in thought, *not* to say 'What's the matter?' or 'Are you all right?' Third, he'd like you not to say anything at all.

The SN difference is regarded as a 'chasm' in the MBTI literature, as the most important source of misunderstanding and conflicts (Bayne, 2004). Some strategies are:

Ss to Ns   Overall picture first, followed by relevant details.
              Emphasize your main point(s). And rather than saying 'It won't work', say 'What would you do about X?'
              Be sparing with detail.

Ns to Ss   Include more detail.
              Say if an idea is only in the beginning stages (and ideally wait until it's more developed).
              Go step by step, starting with a specific statement of the problem.
              Delete some possible solutions.

For example, an ISTJ friend writes detailed and analytic memos, true to her type. My reaction to them is awe at the detail and logic (difference is sometimes attractive, not always a difficulty), but frustration at not knowing, at the start, what they're about. She now adds an opening, general statement to improve her communication with N colleagues.

Myers (1977) recommended starting in the middle if you have a solution which you want to put forward to an N. If you start with the problem, the N is likely to offer a solution which then may get in the way, so start with your idea.

Some strategies for TF are:

Ts to Fs   Try phrasing challenging questions diplomatically.
           Begin with points you agree on if possible.
           Include analysis of any impact on people.
           Remember that Fs need harmony, tend to take criticisms personally, and need to be appreciated.
           Remember how important emotions and morale can be, and that logical analysis sometimes isn't enough.

Fs to Ts   Be direct, concise and calm.
           Give reasons and consequences.
           Remember that criticisms from Ts generally aren't meant personally.
           Remember that Ts *want* their ideas to be critiqued.
           Use assertiveness skills, especially saying no and making requests.
           Remember that harmony is not always possible or even desirable and that Ts tend to focus on problems more than emotions. Don't expect much appreciation.

An example of a subtle difficulty is a T manager taking an MBTI course and as a result complimenting her staff much more on the quality of their work. Some of the staff were less responsive than she'd hoped. They may have been people with a preference for F, who tend to appreciate being complimented more for their personal qualities than their competence.

Some strategies for JP are:

Js to Ps   Trust developed Ps to deliver at the last minute (if they're pressure-prompted Ps – Chapter 2).
           Remember they don't like to be controlled and that they do like to suggest alternatives (Ns too).

Ps to Js   Remember their needs to control, to have plans, to act on plans, and to try to finish well before deadlines.

Another strategy is to describe your own style of working to the other person in a way that respects both your way and theirs. MBTI terms are good for this.

So far I've concentrated on potential communication difficulties between people of opposite preferences. There are two further complications, which can be taken into account to add to effective application. The first is that communicating with people of the same preference as yourself is generally easier, but has its own set of potential problems. In general terms, these are that the strengths of the shared preference can become exaggerated, and that the strengths of the opposite preference can be missed. On the other hand, similarity is also a chance for type development, because someone usually does the things which draw on non-preferences.

The second complication is that each person has four preferences, different degrees of development of each, a dominant function, and a function they generally use in the outside world, i.e. in communicating. Taking all these into account is feasible but sophisticated. For example, an ENFP and an INTJ discuss a shared problem. The ENFP's first reaction is to suggest lots of solutions, the INTJ's is to want to analyse the problem itself. This is a clash of styles best understood as between Introverted N and Extraverted N. In addition, INTJs can sound much more decided about something (TJ) than they actually are (dominant introverted N) and ENFPs can sound much more open than they actually are (dominant extraverted N but their decision-making preference is usually introverted).

However, just the *attempt* to apply MBTI theory at *any* level is likely to aid communication, as are the simplest applications. One of the strongest qualities of MBTI theory is that it's useful at simple levels of application and has deeper levels too.

The best sources of detailed ideas and examples on communication between the psychological types rather than each preference are Tieger and Barron-Tieger (2000), Dunning (2003) and VanSant (2003). Paul Tieger and Barbara Barron-Tieger discuss all combinations of the types in romantic relationships but much of what they say applies to work and other relationships too. They too emphasize that there is no general best combination of types. Rather, it is a matter of how constructive the two or more people can be about their differences. Donna Dunning includes detailed analyses of each type while Sondra VanSant focuses on resolving conflict.

Six contexts

Writing

MBTI theory suggests several approaches to increasing both enjoyment of writing and productivity. A general principle is that standard approaches to helping writers work best for some but that the opposite approach works best for others. An assumption is that each type has a natural writing style (DiTiberio and Jensen, 1995).

I think some of the general literature on improving writing is useful too, though each point may well apply to some types more than others. For example, Boice (1994) studied successful and struggling writers and recommended the following:

1 Give equal time or more to taking notes, and to organizing and playing with them, as to writing, rewriting and editing. Indeed Boice seems to suggest actually defining writing to include taking notes and organizing and playing with them, thus reducing at a stroke the terrors of the blank page and the pressures of 'I must write now'. Easier for Ps?

2 Write little and often. Boice found that 'brief, daily sessions' of ten minutes to an hour are more efficient and more enjoyable (and less draining) than writing for longer periods. Stop before you get tired. Easier for Ps?

3 While writing check how tense you are from time to time and stretch. Easier for Is, Ss and Js?

4 Have realistic expectations, e.g. one and a half to two pages from an hour is good. Other expectations and myths may also get in the way of writing, for example that good writers effortlessly produce flowing prose (when most published writing has been rewritten many times). Easier for Ss?

5 Write a rough draft, and only later be concerned with writing it well. The idea here is to separate writing from editing, and thus reduce interference from the voice that says 'That's not the right word' or 'What sort of a sentence is that?' or, worse, 'I can't write' or 'This is rubbish.' Easier for NFs?

MBTI theory adds two sets of ideas, one (Loomis's approach) an elaboration of the other. Both assume that the most efficient and enjoyable way to write is to use your strengths first, and add the qualities of your non-preferences later.

Some approaches to, and qualities of, good writing (topic and genre aside) are suggested in Exercise 6.6.

Exercise 6.6

Consider which of the following are most true of you now or might come relatively easily to you.

E   Discussing a topic before writing. Fluency and breadth.
I   Immersion in the topic, and depth.
S   Details and concrete examples.
N   Themes and variety of perspective.
T   Analytic style, and criticism.
F   Fluent, expressive style.
J   Focus and stating conclusions.
P   Breadth and revision.

The natural style of each type is a combination of these, with most emphasis on those associated with the dominant function. Conversely, the most troublesome aspects are those associated with the fourth function. The natural style of INFPs, for example, is fluent, in depth, bringing together various themes and perspectives, and happy to revise. INFPs find most trouble with logic, analysis and criticism (T is the fourth function), and also examples and conclusions (S and J).

The recommended strategies for INFPs therefore are to write a first draft as you wish, putting analysis, examples, etc. in only where they come easily, write further drafts in the same way, then revise emphasizing your non-preferences. These are listed separately, in Exercise 6.7, because they sometimes involve cutting back too: for example, Ss may need to reduce the details, Ns to cut some themes and not to bury the main points.

Exercise 6.7

Step 1   Consider whether your writing would be improved by any of the following, or by more attention to them, e.g. If you prefer E would your work be improved by adding the I qualities of more structure and depth?   ▶

E More structure and depth.

I Starting earlier and more breadth.

S Themes and less detail.

N Examples. Fewer ideas.

T More 'signposts', flow, and considering impact on others.

F More analysis, logical order and evidence

J A few more ideas. Some cautious words like 'may'.

P Fewer ideas. A full conclusion.

Step 2 Emphasize your dominant function in a final revision.

Anne Loomis (1999) presented a more elaborate model, focusing on each type's 'writing profile', four stages of writing, techniques for each stage, and ways in which each type can use their preferences in each stage. She called the four stages:

Dreamer
Designer
Builder
Inspector

The Dreamer stage of writing is gathering information and discovering what you want to say. Loomis (1999) recommends techniques such as freewriting, clustering and active imagination. The Designer stage is organizing the information and developing a preliminary outline, a process continued in the Builder stage with definitions, descriptions, images, metaphors, etc. The Inspector stage is refining and editing. I think Loomis's contribution is not in the stages so much as in her ideas about what each stage and technique is like for each psychological type.

Selling and influencing

Exercise 6.8

Step 1 Think of two attempts to sell something to you, one that went well, and one that went badly. ▶

> *Step 2* What do the two attempts suggest about how *you* like to be sold to?
>
> *Step 3* Is how you like to be sold to related to your preferences?

'How do you like to be sold to?' is a key question in Susan Brock's training on psychological type and selling. She asked the question of hundreds of people in several countries and found that STs tend to look for facts, SFs for personalized service, NFs for their vision (in the sense of their ideal) to be supported, and NTs for logical options.

For example, when buying a computer, a customer who prefers ST or who at that moment is in ST mode might ask about memory size, while a customer who's an NT or in NT mode might test your competence or have an explicit set of criteria on which to compare various models of computer. Brock comments that:

> Matching the customer's words, tone and pace, presenting in a manner best suited for a particular type preference, and listening well and exhibiting good product knowledge are all ways to build the relationship – when a relationship has been built, there is often a switch in the customer's perception from 'This sales person in thinking of his or her own needs' to 'This salesperson is thinking of me and what's in my best interest'.

(1994, p. 3)

Brock suggests four stages of selling and that each preference is critical in one or more stages.

1 Initiating the relationship (EI)
2 Investigating needs (S, N, T, F)
3 Suggesting a course of action (S, N, T, F)
4 Obtaining agreement and closing (JP)

Thus, in stage 1 the salesperson can concentrate on matching the other's pace, timing, etc., in stages 2 and 3 their ways of gathering information and making decisions, and in stage 4 their style of closure. For Js this is quicker, for Ps it's more 'No decision before its time.' Brock (1994) gives detailed examples.

Influencing is a broader concept than selling, though related. It includes for example asking for a pay rise and giving feedback to try to improve job performance. In both selling and influencing, knowing what is most and least important to the other person – in part, using their language – is central. Jenny Rogers's (1997) booklet *Influencing Others Using The Sixteen Personality Types* is the key source of guidelines for influencing STs, SFs, NFs, and NTs, and also each of the sixteen types.

Giving and receiving feedback

Giving feedback is another high-level multiple skill, requiring observation, empathy, timing and giving information, each of which is a set of skills itself. An MBTI theory approach to giving feedback to selection interviewers was discussed in Chapter 4, but the skills are relevant to many other aspects of work, especially management.

One idea in this area is that Es are likely to respond to promised rewards, and Is to punishment, or rather to avoid the threat of punishment: carrot or stick?

> Thus extraverted organizations, like those involved in selling, could best motivate and satisfy their staff by providing regular but varied rewards. Equally, a primarily introverted organization, like many bureaucracies, could best shape or motivate staff by the threat of sanctions.
>
> (Furnham and Heaven, 1999, p. 202)

This looks like a theory X approach (Chapter 3) to motivation, and not really sympathetic to MBTI theory. However, it does seem to be true that people differ in their response to rewards and punishments, and I think preferences for T and F are likely to be as relevant as E and I to this difference.

Exercise 6.9

Can you remember examples of when positive feedback felt very good and when it didn't? Can you explain the difference? What do you like to be appreciated for?

I discuss the four styles of leadership proposed by Keirsey (1998), Keirsey and Bates (1973) in Chapter 9. The styles differ markedly on how they tend to appreciate, or not appreciate, their staff, with SPs and NFs readily appreciating others, while SJs and NTs are less comfortable with this. Keirsey and Bates suggest the following guidelines on what to appreciate in staff of different temperaments:

SPs – appreciate recognition of their grace and flair (rather than how much they've done), and of any risks that were involved.

SJs – focus on products, so appreciate being valued for their thoroughness, accuracy and care.

NFs – like appreciation of their unique contribution in a more personal way, of their feelings too, and are not so concerned about the source.

NTs – like appreciation for their ideas and competence. NTs tend to be concerned about the source of the comments; they need to come from someone who they respect as competent to assess them.

A refinement of this framework is to choose words that tend to be powerful for each type, for example:

E	Lively, vital	I	Thoughtful, depth
S	Practical, realistic	N	Original
T	Analytic, systematic	F	Heartfelt, enjoyable
J	Efficient	P	Flexible

Dick Thompson (1999) also offers some constructive ideas about the most useful kinds of feedback for some of the types:

IS Brief, specific. Time to reflect.

ES Recent, specific examples, brief discussions, no written action plan.

IN 'The more visual the feedback the better' (p. 18).

EN Fast-moving.

The general principle here is appreciating people for the best qualities of their temperament. Keirsey and Bates also suggest that SJs and NTs tend to find showing their appreciation of positive feedback difficult.

Conversely, Thompson (1999) suggested the following reactions to *receiving* negative feedback. In summary they (all tendencies):

IS Appear calm outwardly, and attack the next day.

ES Respond immediately.

IN Listen intently and respond the next day.

EN Are flexible. Want to focus on ways to improve.

| IT | Are initially philosophical and attack the next day. |
| ET | React challengingly. |

| IF | Recover slowly. |
| EF | Take it personally and attack. |

Assertiveness

Assertiveness can be defined as 'expressing and acting on your rights as a person while respecting the rights of the other person' (Bayne, 2000; Dickson, 1987). It is thus highly consistent with the aims of MBTI theory and application and is a theory X approach to people at work. The assertive skills which seem to me to be the key ones in organizations are to ask others to do things (making requests), to decide whether to do something or not (saying no), giving compliments and criticisms and receiving compliments and criticisms. Anne Dickson (1987) analyses these skills and others well and her book is for men too, despite its title. The skills are not just techniques; *how* they are used is central. The attitudes and personal qualities of the person using them matter much more than technical virtuosity.

I will take the skills of giving and receiving compliments as an example, for two reasons. First, they are the most clearly related to MBTI theory: Fs, especially FJs, are seen as much more likely to give compliments, and the compliments are most likely to be about the person rather than their work. Fs also want this kind of compliment more. Ts seem to have a different belief about compliments: that they are best used rarely and for exceptional work, but this hasn't been studied empirically as far as I know. I suspect that it's Ts more than Fs who tend to say 'I can't fault X.' Second, because I think there might be important effects on organizational and department morale of unspoken 'rules' like 'Don't ask for positive feedback' and 'Criticize, don't praise.'

Exercise 6.10

Step 1 Can you think of compliments you've given?

Step 2 If not, or only a few, what stops you?

> *Step 3* You may, after considering whether or not you agree with the following arguments and guidelines, like to increase the number of compliments you give.

Books on assertiveness usually include arguments for and against the value of each skill and tips on how to do them. Some reasons for not giving compliments are that you may be seen as manipulative, that the other person knows already that they're valued, that they may get conceited, and that they might put less effort in. Arguments for giving compliments are that they may increase self-esteem, decrease resentment ('the only time I'm noticed is when I do something wrong') and may make negative comments easier to accept.

The basic skill in giving compliments is to be accurate, brief and specific. Genuineness, timing and sensitivity also contribute. A subtle aspect of the skill is that looking for opportunities to give compliments in itself has a positive effect on the person giving compliments. Like other communication skills it is thus much easier as an idea than in practice.

The basic skill of receiving compliments is to thank the other person straightforwardly, and to try not to be dismissive or compliment back quickly. Both reactions can be seen as rejecting the other person's compliment. A refinement of the skill, with a compliment you believe is genuine, is to thank the other person, appreciate it, and then give your view. A refinement with a compliment you're suspicious of is to consider asking for detail, e.g. 'Thank you. Was there anything in particular you liked?' But remember that people who prefer F are less likely to be able to respond analytically at that moment, and yet their compliment can still be genuine.

Team-building

MBTI theory is used to help teams trust and respect each other more, mainly through reframing conflicts and weaknesses as, at best, differences which are valuable when used well or, at worst, differences which are not meant to be irritating or difficult.

A straightforward general framework for MBTI training with a team is:

1 Negotiate a contract.
2 Introduce, complete, score and interpret the MBTI questionnaire.
3 Apply the results to the team.

The contract can include agreeing (if possible) that there *is* a team and what its goals are, and judging whether there is sufficient trust to introduce the MBTI questionnaire. For example, does anyone feel coerced into being there? Other, more standard, elements of the contract concern 'ground rules' like agreeing to listen to each other and (where relevant) confidentiality.

The key issue in the third step is what factors are involved in transferring what is learned to the workplace. Not much is known about this yet. One factor is likely to be having someone in the team (or at least the organization) who is informed and enthusiastic about type, and influential. Another is verifying each members' type well – or, rather, setting the scene for people to verify their own types if they wish. For this reason, it is probably best to have a gap of say two or three weeks between steps two and three. This also gives the consultant more time to design the next step. In practice of course the training may be residential and a block, and trainers either adapt or refer the organization to another consultant.

Some exercises for applying type to teams are:

1 In twos or threes discuss your similarities and differences in type and their effects on you in the team. Report back to the team in terms of strengths and problems of each person.
   Aim: to help each person clarify the impact of their style (type) on others, to value differences more, to practise thinking and talking in MBTI terms. Then, as with the other exercises, apply the problem-solving model (see pp. 157–8).
2 ST, SF, NT and NF groups (or each preference in turn): (1) What do people in your group like to contribute to the team? (2) What do you need from the others?
3 Discuss the team type – usually the most frequently occurring preferences. What strengths and limitations does MBTI theory predict? Any likely sources of friction? What strategies (action plans) might improve the team's effectiveness? More specifically: what about the team type and the team leader's type? Anyone in a minority? (Possible scapegoat). Any preferences missing completely?

4 Groups alike or similar in type make presentations to the team on how they think it can be more effective. This exercise both shows type in action (usually!) and provides some good ideas for the team.

5 Each team member rates the *team* on the following four scales, or variations of them. (This can be done without using the MBTI questionnaire or the team type table. The theory is there of course, but implicit.)

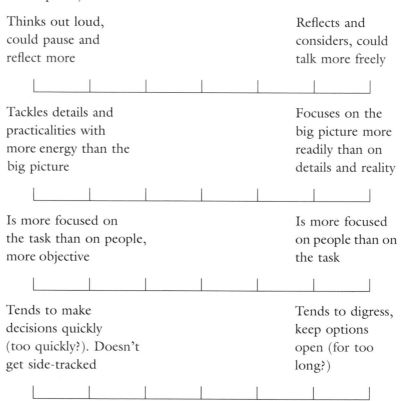

Thinks out loud, could pause and reflect more

Reflects and considers, could talk more freely

Tackles details and practicalities with more energy than the big picture

Focuses on the big picture more readily than on details and reality

Is more focused on the task than on people, more objective

Is more focused on people than on the task

Tends to make decisions quickly (too quickly?). Doesn't get side-tracked

Tends to digress, keep options open (for too long?)

The team discusses the ratings and then, of course, if they would like to change their behaviour and, if so, how. For example, team members may realize that firm plans tend to be vital for Js but stressful for Ps, and that rapidly approaching deadlines tend to be stressful for Js and stimulating for Ps, *and* the implications of this difference for how they treat each other. They become less critical of these differences and look for ways to use them well. Or meetings might include thinking breaks to give introverts (especially) time to reflect. Or an EXTJ team realizes more clearly that their strengths are confidence and a focused, energetic approach but that they are also prone to rushing decisions and overlooking other possibilities.

However, it's also worth bearing in mind that other factors than type may be crucial to a team, e.g. workload. Similarly, other approaches, like FIRO-B, will be better than, or complementary to, the MBTI with some teams and issues. Kwiatkowski and Hogan (1999) give a stimulating general overview of groups and Kummerow and McAllister (1988) and Leonard and Straus (1997) some insightful MBTI case studies.

Steve Myers has recently developed a team roles questionnaire – the MTR-i – which is proving very successful (*www.mtr-i.com*). It measures how much a person is using each preference, or, strictly, each of the eight attitude-functions (IS, ES, etc.). Therefore it can be used to identify inadequate opportunities for use of the dominant function or overuse of the fourth function. However, its main application is identifying sources of conflict within a team, for example the absence of an important role.

Eight team roles are suggested, each related to two psychological types, e.g. the Explorer role and ENTP/ENFP. One of the MTR-i's strengths is that the focus of a workshop on team-building using it can be on the team members and the team, rather than, as can happen with the MBTI questionnaire, on clarifying type.

Research on teams and type suggests that:

> Teams composed of types with similar communication styles seem to perform their tasks quicker, have less conflict, demonstrate greater liking of other team members and listen to one another more than do teams composed of types whose communication style is different.
>
> (Hammer and Huszczo, 1996, p. 97)

So, similarity of type is related to ease and comfort of communication. However, when outcomes are related to type:

> Teams with more diverse communication styles seem to be more effective and to produce outcomes of better quality. This discrepancy seems to be more pronounced when the teams are working on ambiguous versus structured tasks.
>
> (p. 97)

Training

> **Exercise 6.11**
>
> *Step 1*   Think of times when you've learnt about something
>   quickly and enjoyably. Can you say what it was about the
>   teaching method(s) that suited you so well?
>
> *Step 2*   Think of times when you've failed to learn, or learnt only
>   with great effort and in spite of the teaching method.
>   Content aside, can you say what it was about the teaching
>   method(s) that didn't suit you?
>
> *Step 3*   Putting aside, as far as possible, the ways you've been
>   taught, how would you most like to learn?

Unhappy learning experiences seem to be common. Christine Doyle (2003), commenting on research identifying blockages to learning, says that:

> If lifelong learning is to become a reality for the majority, a large number
> of blocks and obstacles have to be overcome first. Perhaps the most
> serious are people's lack of confidence in their own ability to learn and the
> number of damaging misconceptions they hold about effective ways to
> learn.
>
> (p. 236)

MBTI theory focuses on both obstacles and on their application to developing effective training. It suggests that radically different ways of learning tend to suit each type (Lawrence, 1993, 1997). At the least, it gives a wide range of options to try (a level 1 application in the model outlined in Chapter 1). At best it cuts down the guesswork (and suffering) involved in finding which ways of learning are most and least effective for you, and can reduce the chances of someone persisting with a less effective way for them. The styles vary dramatically. For example, brainstorming, which is so popular among trainers, is as natural as breathing for some types, but pointless and threatening to others.

The ideas about learning style listed next are at the level of the preferences, but as usual a further assumption is that the dominant function is the most important. For example an ET learning style is one of action and analysis. This is *not* to say that ETs need continual action and analysis and nothing else, but that this is the emphasis which tends to suit ETs best. These ideas are adapted from Jensen, 1987; DiTiberio and Hammer, 1993 and Lawrence, 1997.

E   Action, talk, trial and error, group projects.

I   Reflection, work privately.

S   Close observations of what actually happens. Start with the concrete and specific, with ideas and theory later. Specific directions. Step by step.

N   Theory first. Links and possibilities. Surges of interest. Imaginative leaps. Brainstorming.

T   Analysis and logic. Critiques. Logic. Systems. Flow charts.

F   Harmonious atmosphere. Need to care about the topic.

J   More formal. Organized. Clear expectations and criteria.

P   Flexible. Not routine. Bursts of energy. Work as play. Learning as a 'free-wheeling, flexible quest' (Jensen, 1987, p. 186).

The teaching methods most compatible with each learning style are obvious. The problems are that generally only some of the methods can realistically be available in one session, and that trainers have preferred styles too. However, it is still useful for trainees and trainers to know their styles and their effects on others.

Mismatches in terms of type between training and learning styles are inevitable. STs for example tend to want practical, detailed information while NFs prefer general impressions, patterns and possibilities. A solution is to continue predominantly with your own style but add some flexibility. (Jung referred to teachers falsifying their type as 'educational monstrosities', Jensen, 1987 p. 88.) Thus, Introverted lecturers could allow more time for discussion, Ns include more facts (while concentrating on theories and concepts), Ts praise as well as challenge, and so on.

Similarly, trainees can be offered choices of exercises (primarily in S and N formats) and a choice of how to work on them (allowing for E and I). As Gordon Lawrence puts it: 'We can find teaching styles that accommodate the essential needs of our own types and at the same time provide a good learning environment for students of other types' (1993, p. 58).

The following results from an unpublished interview study by L. L. Thompson (cited Lawrence, 1993, pp. 77–9) may evoke a shock of recognition. They are concerned with differences in planning a course. Several other aspects of teaching were studied, including where ideas for teaching come from and what feels successful, with similarly strong results. For planning, the findings, which echo Brock's views on selling discussed earlier, were:

ST Detailed plans with specific objectives.

SF Detailed plans taking students' abilities into account.

NF Plans structured around general goals, themes and students' needs, adapting the plans as the course unfolds.

NT Overall structure organized by concepts or themes.

Conclusions

A major application of MBTI theory is to improve communication through the 'constructive use of differences'. The theory suggests ways of preventing clashes, conflicts and misunderstandings. It also explains, at least in part, some clashes and suggests strategies for trying to resolve them. Areas for application include writing, where a main principle is to use your preferences first and revise with your non-preferences; selling and influencing; giving and receiving feedback; assertiveness; team building; and training.

7 Health

In many organizations, to get ahead you need to be fit, or at least to look fit. This chapter reviews some ideas from MBTI theory and research about four areas of health which are related to being fit: exercise, eating, physical illness, specifically coronary heart disease (CHD) and chronic lower back pain, and stress. In a recent survey of nearly 16000 European workers, 29 per cent said that their work had an adverse effect on their health, with back pain (30 per cent), and stress (28 per cent), the problems cited most often (Le Blanc *et al.*, 2000). The direct and indirect costs of sickness absence are said to be enormous – billions of pounds in the UK alone (Le Blanc *et al.*, 2000). I think MBTI theory can, on current knowledge, be useful in prevention and treatment, therefore potentially increasing job performance and reducing staff absence.

Physical activity

Some people have no wish to do the recommended amount of physical activity and some survive well without it. This section may not be for you or of course for those happy with their fitness levels. On the other hand, the definition of healthy physical activity – keeping fit – has broadened recently (reflected in the wider use of the term 'physical activity' instead of 'exercise') and there are some new ideas about it which may be worth a quick check, especially as most contemporary western work makes much more use of our minds than our bodies.

The first question about physical fitness is: what do you want to be fit for? If it is for everyday life rather than a sport, only what is called a 'comfortable level' of physical activity is needed. The recommendations from the Center for Disease Control in the US have changed from sweaty and out of breath for twenty minutes, three times a week, to more frequent, lower intensity activity like walking and climbing stairs, and aiming to *accumulate* about thirty minutes of this most days (Wimbush, 1994). More than thirty minutes, or more vigorous exercise, gives a reserve of fitness and probably more protection against some diseases, but is seen as an extra rather than necessary (Wimbush, 1994; Seligman, 1995). A second question – how much exercise is too much? – seems to be a problem for only a few people (Cockerill and Riddington, 1996).

Thayer's research (1987, 1996) on mild exercise and its effects on mood supports the effectiveness of fairly brisk ten-minute walks. They increase energy and reduce tension for the next two hours on average. Music was also reported as quite effective (so dancing might be particularly beneficial). The main principle if you want to take on more demanding forms of exercise is gradually and comfortably to be more active. 'Comfortably' implies a judgement based on S and F, radically different from an external criterion like number of miles or minutes.

Exercise 7.1

Step 1 Which physical activities have you tried and stopped? Which activities are you repelled by? Which appeal to you?

Step 2 Do you see any connections between these activities and attitudes and MBTI theory?

Step 3 Taking into account the suggestions below are there any new physical activities or settings, or familiar activities done in a new way or in a new setting, that seem worth trying?

MBTI theory suggests that some forms of physical activity and some approaches to it tend to suit each psychological type. They will then be more enjoyable and easier to sustain for people of those types, as many people start a physical activity with drive and enthusiasm, but it doesn't last. The following suggestions and hypotheses are adapted from Wennik (1999), Brue (2003) and other sources:

S   Demonstrations (tapes, classes) and quite quick results

N   Different and unusual
Variety
Able to change activities easily
Create own programme

T   Increasing competence
Competent, gratified instructor

F   Enjoyable
Praised
Warm instructor who's interested in you

And, in terms of dominant functions:

ES   Lively and stimulating in a sensory way
Quick responses needed
Variations on the familiar rather than completely new

IS   Doing it the right way
Routine and safe

EN   Efficient and stimulating
Variety

IN   Interesting
Repetition – allowing mental drift
Safety

ET   Structured
Routine
Disciplined

IT   Efficiency and increasing competence
Interest in underlying principles

EF   Friendly groups
Attractive surroundings

IF   Individual meaning or philosophy

Most contemporary western work involves lots of sitting so I've included an exercise for waists. It's from an old book (Morehouse and Gross, 1977) but I've checked with a physiotherapy lecturer that it's safe and consistent with current thinking. Check with a doctor, physiotherapist or osteopath first though that it's safe for you. Sit-backs, according to Morehouse and Gross (1977) are an easier, safer and more effective way of strengthening stomach muscles than the better known sit-ups.

1 Sit on the floor with your feet held by someone or under a heavy piece of furniture and your knees bent and comfortably close to your chest.

2 Move your back towards the floor until you feel your stomach muscles working (this may be a few inches at first). Hold at this point for 15–20 seconds and return to the starting position and rest. Do this at your own rhythm for about two minutes. Rest with your arms on the floor or holding your knees.

3 If your muscles start to quiver you've gone too far back. Work towards 20 seconds before the quivering starts. Your body is telling you what it can comfortably do. Similarly, try one set of sit-backs a day at first and increase them at a comfortable rate.

4 Keep breathing as you do the sit-backs.

5 If you decide to go so far as to hold a sit-back for 20 seconds with your back brushing the floor, you may or may not wish to make it even more difficult by putting your arms behind your head, holding for longer or holding a weight on your chest.

Another method is to tighten your stomach muscles as you walk, starting with a few steps, then relaxing, and building up comfortably and gradually. For preventive and healing exercises for backs and necks, see McKenzie (1983, 1988) and *www.backcare.org.uk*. Again, check with a doctor, physiotherapist or osteopath first.

Eating

The relationship between eating and health generally means two things: eating to lose or maintain weight, and eating in a nutritious way to maintain good energy levels, prevent illness and aid recovery from illness. Happily, in practice the two aims are most likely to be achieved by eating the same foods. However, this is not to say that it's easy. I'll discuss losing weight as it's the more difficult of the two, and a concern for more than half the general UK population.

Several factors affect body weight and make discrimination against people who are 'overweight' unfair. For example, our evolutionary history means that as a species we're much better at coping with scarcity than resisting abundance. So when we eat more calories than we need, we store them as fat, but when we eat fewer calories than we need, our bodies turn our metabolic rate down. Physical activity raises the rate, but if you haven't eaten well you probably don't have enough energy. Genetic factors play a part, further contradicting the attitude that obesity is a sign of weakness and of being out of control. Historically, thin has rarely been seen as the most desirable body shape (Klein, 1997). Rather, social attitudes have varied enormously, with the current 'very' slim perhaps due to be replaced by 'more rounded' or, ideally, by greater acceptance of diversity, and soon.

Obesity is a major cause of ill health and premature death (Brownell and Rodin, 1994) but many people who are distressed or unhappy about their weight are not obese. Assuming that weight loss for a particular person is desirable (which can be a big and questionable assumption) there are many controversies about how to achieve it: low carbohydrates or lots of carbohydrates; low fat or lots of fat; good fat versus bad fat; 'grazing' versus proper meals; and of course a vast, confusing and highly profitable array of recommended diets which may or may not be harmful and/or effective.

However, we do know quite a lot that's useful about weight loss and it seems clear that the most effective way, generally speaking, is to eat a well-balanced and varied diet, eat a little less, and be a little more active physically, and *gradually* (a pound or two a week) lose weight. That's 26 or 52 pounds in six months!

MBTI theory contributes some ideas about *how* to eat less. It suggests a wider range of strategies for losing weight than are generally considered, and further that some of these are more likely to be effective with some psychological types. The strategies have been linked to the temperaments (Kroeger, 1985; Scanlon, 1986) and to the preferences, especially JP (Scanlon, 1986; Wennik, 1999).

Susan Scanlon sees SPs as more 'in touch with' feeling hungry and full, and therefore less likely to need or want to lose weight. This skill can be developed by focusing attention on 'Am I hungry?', 'What exactly do I want to eat?', and 'Do I really want to eat more now?' Type theory predicts though that, because it is part of Introverted Sensing, SJs would develop the skill much more readily than others. Moreover, the types least likely to have developed it are the dominant Intuitives, especially ENTPs and ENFPs.

The other guidelines suggested by Scanlon are straightforwardly consistent with MBTI theory. Thus, SPs, who tend to find plans frustrating, can try a 'sort of' diet, with lots of variety and flexibility. They can stock up with healthy and mainly low-calorie food and enjoy choosing at the time; try to eat a bit less than usual; and (probably a necessary rule because SPs tend to be low on controlling impulses), don't keep many high-calorie foods at home. These ideas probably apply to Ps generally as well.

In contrast, SJs are expected to respond well to traditional strategies for losing weight: to detailed rules and plans, applied with discipline and responsibility. Thus, meals can be planned a week ahead, perhaps in measured portions as well, and records kept of food eaten and weight lost.

Because NTs like analysis, design and solving problems, their most effective strategies are likely to be studying theory and designing their own strategies. They are likely to also need to develop a strategy for actually acting on the knowledge.

NFs' main motives are self-development and helping others. They also need compliments most – or perhaps it's more a matter of responding least well to criticism. Otto Kroeger (1985) suggested that NFs are the most likely to overeat from guilt or unhappiness, and that this – rather than food itself – should be the first focus. Support groups or friends could play a prominent role here. Also, losing weight for someone else could appeal to this temperament particularly. Overall, the general 'flavour' for NFs is co-operating with one's body rather than controlling it, and 'feeling right'.

I'll also mention some simple general ideas which have proved helpful to some people regardless of psychological type:

- Chew more/eat more slowly.
- Taste your food.
- When you feel like eating, try drinking water first; you might only be thirsty.
- If you eat small amounts towards the end of the day, you'll wake up really hungry, which can lead to enjoying breakfast more.
- Sleep enough for you (so that – ideally – you don't need an alarm clock and wake feeling rested). Restless nights could be seen as good for weight loss because they use up calories but they actually have the *opposite* effect: cortisol is released which encourages fat.

- Periods of four or five hours without eating give your liver a rest.
- Emphasize adding healthy foods more than avoiding less healthy ones.

Roberta Wennik (1999) lists several reasons for people eating when they're not hungry (pp. 146–7), and then reviews them in terms of MBTI theory, first explaining the reason, usually involving the dominant or auxiliary preferences, and then challenging it directly, using different preferences. For example: 'My friend made this cake for me.' A common reason for eating it is not to hurt the friend's feelings (mainly an F reason, to preserve harmony). A T perspective is that it's illogical, and an N perspective that you could take a bite and save the rest for later.

Generally, I think the challenges suggested by Wennik could work well, e.g. 'I deserve it as a reward for being so good' can be challenged by using N to suggest alternative rewards, and T to tell yourself that when food is used frequently as a reward there are costs. And 'It was free' can be challenged by using T to consider the consequences, S to ask if you're really hungry for the particular food and F to ask how important 'getting something for nothing' is in your core values.

The overall strategy in these examples is to use two or more of the functions – S, N, T or F – to break, or at least impede, bad habits. Faced with an eating decision, you can consult each of the functions:

1 Your S function. Am I really hungry? If not, what is it about this situation that inclines me to eat? Is it for example the time, the smell, wanting to please (or not to risk displeasing) someone, comfort, boredom, a difficult emotion, thirst …?
2 Your N function. Imagine meeting the need in another way.
3 Your T function. If you eat when you're not hungry, the extra calories will be stored as fat. What are the arguments for and against the alternatives?
4 Your F function. Which of your core values are the most salient here?

Remember that the best decisions are made using all four functions, as in the later section in this chapter on expressive writing and the model of managing problems in Chapter 9.

Physical illness

The main personality characteristics that have been shown to affect health are hostility, neuroticism and optimism (Smith and Spiro, 2002). Of these, hostility, which refers to cynicism, aggressiveness and mistrust, is the most clearly relevant to MBTI theory. It is associated with T, but only in an extreme form and when there is also poor development of F. Smith and Spiro criticize the conceptual clarity of 'hostility' and problems with measuring it, but nevertheless conclude that the research 'represents perhaps the strongest finding regarding personality and subsequent disease' (p. 378). The 'disease' in this conclusion is CHD (and early death).

Part of the explanation for the relationship between CHD and hostility appears to be that hostile people respond to stressful situation with larger increases in blood pressure, heart rate, etc. than other people do. They also respond less well physiologically to social support, which they receive less of anyway, and have more unhealthy habits including smoking and inactivity.

Studies of psychological type and CHD were reviewed by John Shelton (1996). They suggest that ISTJs and ISFJs are more prone to CHD than other types. In particular 'The frequency of ISTJs among CHD patients is four times what would be expected' (p. 203). However, there is much that is not known about the causes of CHD, and such figures strike a cautionary note and no more than that.

For chronic low back pain, the opposite pattern, in some respects, to CHD is suggested: it is INFPs who tend to be over-represented in patients who report the most difficulties (Shelton, 1996). Part of the problem seems to be *overdoing*: 'impulsive, spontaneous and poorly controlled bursts of activity that often cause flare-ups in the cycle of pain' (pp. 207-8). Ps seem to be the most prone to this error.

MBTI theory has been used to help people with other chronic illnesses cope better. Ron Penner (1992) worked with support groups of people suffering from Chronic Fatigue Syndrome. He found the JP preference particularly helpful. Js who coped most successfully with the major loss of control that this illness brings reported a 'shift of gears' and accepting less control in their lives, while Ps who coped best built *more* structure into theirs. Penner also found that EPs had most trouble adapting because their minds need such a high level of external stimulation and their bodies need the opposite. Then, when they do rest more, they get bored.

Using temperament theory, he hypothesized:

that SJs will tend to focus on their decreased ability to meet their responsibilities, duties, and obligations; SPs might focus on decrements in physical capabilities, recreational activities, coordination, and balance. NTs ... are more likely to focus on cognitive changes, their sense of competence, and searching for the 'why' of their symptoms. NFs might worry more about the future, the disastrous possibilities that it entails, and the impact on loved ones.

(p. 16)

Thus, Penner's main idea for using MBTI theory in helping patients cope with chronic illness is to take into account the core needs that are not being met, and to try to help the person adapt accordingly.

Stress

Stress is a very widely used word in everyday life and a problem for most of us. Questionnaire surveys suggest that 25 per cent of the population are 'often' or 'always' stressed – which seems an extraordinarily high figure. The high sales of *The Little Book of Calm* and other books on coping with stress provide indirect evidence of high levels of stress. Quite a lot is known about the general causes and consequences of stress and about ways of coping with it (Cooper *et al.* 2001; Jones and Bright, 2001; Doyle, 2003), so it is quite surprising that stress appears to be increasing. There is thought to be an enormous cost to western economies, e.g. an average 10 per cent of gross national product spent by European countries on the consequences of job stress (Cartwright and Cooper, 1996).

A useful working definition of 'stress' is 'the experience of unpleasant over- or under-stimulation, as defined by the individual in question, that actually or potentially leads to ill health' (Bond, 1986). Jones and Bright (2001) review other definitions. Meg Bond's definition recognizes the fact that different people find radically different things stressful and it has a flavour of feeling strained to the extent of feeling overwhelmed, as in everything being 'too much to bear' (too much stimulation) or 'going out my mind with boredom' (too little).

The definition also includes a statement about the effects of stress on health, a controversial field discussed well by Sapolsky (1998). Several illnesses are also thought by most researchers in the area to be caused by chronic stress or made worse by it, for example, asthma, heart disease, headaches. Stress does alter immune function, through hormones and through depriving the immune system of energy, but is probably a minor factor in ill health compared to diet, smoking, poverty, genetic factors, etc., though still worth attention. It has been shown to contribute to colds and to slow down the healing of wounds for example (e.g. Cohen *et al.*, 1998).

Most definitions of stress emphasize the role of individuals rather than their organizations, social contexts or cultures. However, if the organization, for example, is too cold, too demanding or too hostile, then the organization itself is arguably the main source of stress and interventions for managing stress will be most effective at that level. For example, the organization could reduce its demands on employees and discuss with them ways of increasing their sense of control (rather than just providing stress-management workshops or an EAP). On the other hand, it is probable that each of us as an individual contributes significantly to our own level of stress.

In the following sections, I outline a three-stage model of coping with stress, discuss type and signs, sources and strategies, and discuss the coping strategy of expressive writing.

The ideas discussed apply to everyday stress rather than what Buyssen (1996) calls psychotraumatic stress. He recommends asking for professional help when other strategies have failed or when, after a traumatic event, any of the following apply:

- your emotions are too intense, and you feel chronically tense and empty;
- your symptoms do not disappear, e.g. lack of appetite, nightmares;
- one of more of the three main elements of psychotrauma, i.e. re-experiencing, denial and inappropriate arousal, persists;
- after a month, you are still not able to enjoy anything.

Coping with stress

A three stage model for coping with stress is:

Stage 1   Monitor your signs of too much or too little stress, especially early warnings

Stage 2 Choose one or more strategies

Stage 3 Try them out, monitoring the effects

Signs of stress

Exercise 7.2

How do you as an individual experience too much or too little stress and, in particular, what are the early signs?

Some of the more common effects or signs of too much or too little stress are:

On thoughts and emotions
- difficulty concentrating
- anxious
- 'tired all the time'
- bored
- depressed
- lonely

On the body
- tight throat
- sweating
- dry mouth
- tics
- frequent urinations
- aches

On behaviour
- irritable
- critical
- accidents
- drugs
- difficulties in sleeping
- eat less/more

It is important to note that some of these signs may be caused by illness rather than stress and need medical attention.

I think temperament theory is clearest on people's different reactions to stress. Some ideas, adapted from unpublished work by Valerie Stewart, are:

Reactions to stress

SP Frivolity, flight, 'go own way', breakdown

SJ Redefine objectives, more resources, double check, more control, dogmatic

NT Overwork, fight, intolerance, conform rebelliously, pedantic debate

NF Self-sacrifice, cynicism, hysteria, depression

Exercise 7.3

Ask people who know you well how they know when you're stressed, especially the earliest signs.

You may already be skilled at noticing when you are becoming stressed. However, improvement in your monitoring may be possible through asking others how they know when you're stressed and by self-observation (difficult though this can be). You may, for example, find that a tight mouth or a twitching eye (both signs of muscle tension) are reliable early warnings for you, but that an observant colleague uses the way you speak as her own clue about you. Some people – perhaps SPs – will be more skilful at observing such clues, but most people can improve. It is also quite likely that each type will tend to have 'favourite' signs but the research hasn't been done yet.

One sign of stress, unfortunately, is ignoring such signs. Ideally, each person will notice *early* signs of stress and take action to reduce or remove them. The advantages of early action are obvious: less energy wasted and less damage done. Working out the cause(s) or stressors may also be more feasible, and the effects are less likely to become chronic.

Sources of stress

Organizations, and life generally, are often seen as increasingly stressful in western culture: downsizing, outsourcing, mergers, job insecurity, new technology, longer working hours (in the UK), sleep deprivation, workplace bullying, etc. (e.g. Sparks *et* al., 2001; Doyle, 2003). It's a bleak picture, apparently at odds with the typically high levels of job satisfaction reported (Chapter 3), and often lacking a world or historical perspective. However, levels of stress *are* high and factors like work overload can be impossible for anyone, of any psychological type, to cope with. MBTI theory therefore offers some ideas about part of a very complex problem.

Some ideas about temperament and sources of stress adapted from unpublished work by Valerie Stewart, are:

SP Not much happening. Monotony. Unclear or no information. Lack of Freedom. (Unclear objectives matter much less.)

SJ Unclear objectives. Changes of plan. Ambiguity. Lack of control.

NT Doing routine and repetitive things, especially if they're detailed as well. Bureaucracy. Difficult relationships.

NF Conflict. Saying no. Depressed and suicidal people. Criticism.

Coping strategies

Exercise 7.4

List your current strategies regardless of whether they're good or bad. Indeed, it is hard to judge most coping strategies in an absolute way. Physical activity, for example, can be the wrong kind for someone or can become obsessive.

There are many classifications of coping strategies, e.g. mind, emotions, body and 'spirit', and 'problem-focused' versus 'emotion-focused', with no agreement as yet on which is the most useful (O'Driscoll and Cooper, 1996). A four-part classification is:

1 Reduce the effects of stress
  • relaxation
  • play/fun
  • massage
  • exercise (short-term)
  • meditation

2 Increase self-awareness (with a view to action)
- talk/write
- support groups
- counselling
- uncover, challenge and replace irrational beliefs
- clarify values
- develop other assertive qualities and skills

3 Discover situational causes (and consider dealing with them directly or changing your attitude towards them).

4 Build up physical and emotional resilience: diet, exercise (long-term), Sleep, etc.

Stage 2 of the three-stage model is choosing one or more strategies. For example, I noticed that I was biting my lip shortly after a colleague had spoken to me (stage 1). I checked through some strategies and decided to (1) deliberately relax physically – I did some stretching, (2) talk to a friend about the situation and my reaction, and (3) look for an irrational belief. I found that my colleague was not (this time) the primary cause of my stress, and that an irrational belief was, or seemed to be: that 'people are not allowed to change their minds' when, of course they are, even on the particular decision! What mattered most, though, was that I looked after myself by trying to clarify what had happened, first through observation and then through specific, realistic actions. There can be a subtle effect here: relatively minor changes leading to greater motivation, and then to more changes – the opposite of a spiral decline.

A good principle from MBTI theory is to try something that is comfortable for you first, then, if necessary or if you wish, to try something else. For example:

E	To talk
I	To reflect
S	A sensory activity
N	To design something new
T	To feel competent, to analyse and challenge
F	Harmony
J	A plan for finishing something
P	Flexibility and autonomy

More subtly, Kroeger with Thuesen (1992) also suggest that sometimes the most effective strategy is to seek balance by using the opposite preference, though perhaps only briefly (p. 247). Obviously, this recommendation can be seen as trying to 'have it both ways'; however, I think they're recognizing the complexities of type and particularly type development. The 'good stretches' are:

E   Take notes, write
I   Intimate, spontaneous talk

S   Fantasize
N   Do something sensory/detailed

T   Empathize
F   Analyse something

J   Abandon the schedule
P   Plan something and do it

There is a lot of research on the main causes of stress in different occupations, on ways of thinking about and measuring coping with stress, and on the effectiveness of different strategies. Much of this, like the work on stress and illness, is still at a fairly early stage – theory and conjecture rather than based on good evidence. We are not yet justified in saying, 'This technique has been shown the most likely to be effective with this kind of problem and for the kind of person you are.' Rather, it is a matter of discussing options and the obstacles to achieving them, taking some useful findings into account and then individual experimentation and follow-up.

Finally, the approach to coping with stress discussed so far works much of the time. However, sometimes there are deeper, motivational problems. Why does X who knows all the arguments continue to overwork and ignore her feelings of futility and emptiness? Why does Y, who knows all the arguments and wants to eat more healthily and exercise, do quite well for a few days and then, as he sees it, fail again? Theories of change and motivation, and counselling and coaching, suggest various explanations and options to try, but the next section is about a strategy that is generally effective, but which it may be useful to refine using MBTI theory.

Expressive writing

I've included writing as a coping strategy for several reasons: (a) it illustrates the three-stage model well; (b) the evidence for its effectiveness is unusually good (although individual differences have not been studied yet); (c) it is not usually included in books on stress management; (d) there are no contra-indications yet, which there are for nearly all the other strategies, even physical relaxation; (e) it is very inexpensive, portable and private, and (f) it can be used to clarify motives for *not* looking after yourself.

Spera *et al.'s* (1994) study is an example of the approach and its effectiveness. They asked unemployed professionals either to write about their reactions to redundancy (experimental group) or about relatively superficial matters (control group). Those in the experimental group found new jobs more quickly, although not because they applied for more jobs or wrote more letters. The most likely explanations are a gain in perspective and sense of control, and less energy used in suppressing troubling thoughts and emotions. Rumination – being preoccupied with an emotional upset, when it goes 'round and round' and dominates – seems to be particularly stressful, and expressive writing may also work through reducing it. A further explanation is that writing may help the writer to sort out what matters most and decide what can wait, be delegated or discarded. A 'sense of control' seems to be central to this explanation (Sparks *et al.*, 2001).

The main researcher in this area is James Pennebaker (e.g. Pennebaker *et al.*, 1990) and the main and firm general finding is that writing about stressful events tends to have both psychological benefits and health benefits (Smyth, 1998). Inevitably there are questions about it, for example: What factors are related to these effects? Is it damaging for some people? Does it make counselling and coaching redundant?

The next section applies MBTI theory to an approach to expressive writing consistent with Pennebaker's.

The approach has three stages: write freely, analyse, and act.

Stage 1: Write freely – not analysing and not concerned with literary merit – about a troubling problem or 'event'.

Alternatively, freewrite. This means writing without stopping, even if it means writing say 'This is a waste of time, I can't think what to write', and for at least ten minutes. **Write anything but keep writing**.

Stage 1 requires use of the preference for I and this first variation explicitly bans T.

Freewriting was developed to treat writer's block (Elbow, 1997) and ten minutes is the shortest length of time used in research on expressive writing.

Stage 2: Analyse what you've written, using some of the following questions:

(a) Might it be useful to be more specific about any aspects?
(b) What is the evidence for any assertions, beliefs?
(c) Are there any familiar feelings or patterns here?
(d) Am I making any assumptions?
(e) Do my reactions tell me anything about myself, for example, suggest important values or principles?
(f) How realistic am I being?
(g) What other ways (however unlikely) are there of looking at what happened and how I reacted?

Stage 2 requires I throughout, S for questions (a) and (f), N for (c), (d) and (g), T for (d) and (e), and F for (e).

Stage 3: Consider possible actions.

Action can be doing something or changing an attitude. In terms of the preferences, Stage 3 is open, but E and J are required if you decide to act in the sense of doing something.

An example of the whole model is:

Stage 1: *Write freely*

I was furious. How can he give me *more* work *and* not ask me first. I've got too much to do already. But it was that half-smile and look away that really got to me. I think he knew exactly what he was doing. Perhaps he wants me to leave. Perhaps it's revenge or putting me in my place. Well he can sod off. I just won't do it and see what he does then.

Stage 2: *Analysis*

What I actually said to X was 'This sort of thing makes me feel like leaving'. I said it angrily but not abusively. I don't *know* what his motives were. I resent most being told what to do as if I was a servant. Autonomy is very important to me. He may have been embarrassed to ask me to do more when he doesn't ask Z. I'm glad I reacted spontaneously and strongly. Now I feel calmer, the extra work has some positive possibilities (though I'd still much rather not do it).

Stage 3: *Possible actions*

Talk to A and B about it. Ask for their views.
Accept that it's not worth a fight – probably.
Nor is the insult – the 'servant' part. I don't trust X enough, at least at the moment. On the other hand, it doesn't take any trust to say something to him about consultation. Think about how to put it.
Think about what to put less effort into or postpone/cancel, in order to do the new work.
Check how realistic the positive possibilities are.
Note my characteristic reaction to being ordered about and talk/write about it.

Evaluation of the example

The process has worked well. There is reasonable awareness of emotions. The writer shows some commitment to pursue related 'patterns' – is not just preoccupied by his immediate problem. The possible actions seem realistic but they could be stated more specifically, for example, when will the writer talk to A and B? The writer has used some of questions (a) to (g) in stage 2, and the general shape and process are consistent with the model. MBTI theory suggests that he could usefully consider putting more effort into the elements of the model which call on his non-preferences, especially T.

A note on work–life balance

Work–life balance seems to be generally regarded as a good thing, but, from an MBTI perspective, it depends. The problem is that some types thrive on structure, and benefit from boundaries between work and leisure, while others, as much as possible, treat work as play and therefore don't distinguish between life and work much of the time. For the first group (mainly Js) life–work balance may well be an issue; for the second group (mainly Ps), provided they're in a job that suits them, I suspect it isn't.

Conclusions

MBTI theory suggests that attempts to eat or exercise healthily are more likely to work if the method matches (or is at least not strongly opposed to) your psychological type. The reason is that they will be easier to sustain. Similarly, each type is more likely to be helped by a different approach to coping with chronic illness and with stress. Sources of stress, reactions to stress and effective coping strategies are all radically different. A strategy which is quite generally effective – expressive writing – may be usefully refined by the theory.

8   Counselling and coaching

In the last few years there has been a 'huge expansion' (Doyle, 2003) in the role of counselling at work. Its most obvious uses are career development and helping employees manage or resolve problems that are interfering with their work. Helping people cope with redundancy is a less obvious use, but one that makes good business sense (Herriot and Pemberton, 1995). Coaching is expanding very fast too, and overlaps considerably with counselling in several respects (Bayne *et al.*, 2003).

In this chapter I first touch on two general issues: the effectiveness of workplace counselling, and whether or not there are any significant differences between counselling, coaching, psychotherapy and other related activities. Then I focus in turn on applications of MBTI theory to eight aspects of counselling and coaching: (1) a general framework for counselling and coaching, (2) the core qualities of empathy, respect and genuineness, (3) listening, (4) choice of orientation, (5) choice of strategies and techniques, (6) choice of ways of presenting techniques, (7) the 'authentic chameleon' issue and (8) a perspective on how much people can change. All the areas of application discussed can be related to the following general questions, each of which can therefore be informed by type:

1 What does this potential client want?
2 Am I the right person for him or her?
3 If so, how are we going to work together?

The fundamental issue of whether or not counselling works has been resolved (Hubble *et al.*, 1999; Orlans, 2003). The finding that most approaches work most of the time supports a common factors explanation but we don't fully understand *how* it works. For example, there are many common factors such as empathy, encouraging hope and readiness to change, and we don't know which are the crucial ones. The *relationship* between counsellor and client is probably the main factor, but it too is complex, and therefore raises many possibilities and questions. Similarly the term, empathy, is used in different ways and has various meanings (Duan and Hill, 1996). Churchill and Bayne (1998) showed that MBTI theory clarifies these different conceptions of empathy. For example, experienced counsellors who preferred T and J had a more active conception of empathy than those who preferred F and P.

Exercise 8.1

What words and images do you associate with 'counsellor' and 'coach'? What about 'psychotherapist' and 'mentor'?

The second general issue is the differences, if any, between the activities or roles in Exercise 8.1. There have been many attempts to distinguish between two or more of them (McLeod, 2003) but no agreement. I think there are considerable overlaps (at least) between them in several central respects: the theories on which they are based, the processes involved, the methods and techniques used, and the goals sought (Bayne *et al.*, 2003). One clear difference is image, hence the exercise. Coaching is more socially acceptable than counselling in some circumstances, and it would be interesting to know when and where this is so.

Two kinds of coaching can be distinguished: business or executive coaching which focuses on helping people improve their performance at work, and life coaching, which is more general, and includes helping people become more assertive or lead a healthier lifestyle. 'Life strategist' is a new name for the second kind of coach. Here too there is considerable overlap. Obviously, work problems are sometimes related to other aspects of life and vice versa.

MBTI theory suggests that the psychological type of each counsellor and coach is a factor in their comfort and effectiveness with the various orientations, styles, stages and skills. However, there is a marked bias in counselling and perhaps in coaching towards preferences for F (dealing with people) and N (inferring meanings). This does *not* mean that other types should avoid being counsellors or coaches: all the types can be good counsellors and coaches, but with different patterns of comfort and strengths, as reviewed in the rest of this chapter.

A general framework for counselling and coaching

MBTI theory is most consistent with an integrative framework for counselling, with empathy at its heart. The framework outlined below is a variation of Gerard Egan's widely used Skilled Helper Model (e.g. Egan, 2002), especially its earlier, simpler versions. Clara Hill and Karen O'Brien (1999) and others have also proposed very similar frameworks.

Stage one: Explore

The counsellor/coach accepts and empathizes with their client and is genuine. The client explores her or his emotions, thoughts, behaviour and experiences related to a problem or goal. This stage calls most for I, S, F and P strengths.

Stage two (if necessary): Understand

The counsellor/coach suggests, or helps their client to suggest, themes and patterns and new ways of looking at a problem. This stage calls for N and T strengths in addition to those of stage one.

Stage three (if necessary): Act

The counsellor/coach helps the client decide what action to take (if any), taking costs and benefits for self and others into account, and evaluating the results. This stage calls for E and J strengths, in addition to those of stages one and two.

This framework is a conceptual map and guide which enables the counsellor or coach to locate where they are in a session or with a particular issue. The sessions themselves will be fluid, moving backwards and forwards between the stages. The stages and skills associated with them are all strengths of particular preferences, and almost in the order of the standard type formula (Table 8.1). The strengths and corresponding 'likely aspects to work on' (or weaknesses) listed in Table 8.1 can also be used to develop and analyse counselling qualities and skills.

Table 8.1	**Strengths and aspects to work on for counsellors and coaches**	
	Likely strengths	Likely aspects to work on
E	Helping clients explore a wide range of issues Easy initial contact Thinking 'on feet'	Using silence Helping clients explore issues in sufficient depth Reaching the action stage too early
I	Helping the client explore a few issues in depth Reflecting on strategies, etc. Using silence	Helping clients move to action Helping clients explore all relevant issues Ease of initial contact
S	Observing details Being realistic Helping clients decide on practical action plans	Taking the overall picture into account Brainstorming (strategies, challenges, and actions) Using hunches
N	Seeing the overall picture Brainstorming Using hunches	Being specific Testing hunches Helping clients decide on practical action plans
T	Being objective Challenging (i.e., from the counsellor's or coach's frame of reference)	'Picking up' feelings Being empathic (i.e., in client's frame of reference) Being warmer Challenging in a timely way (not prematurely)
F	Being warm Being empathic	Taking thoughts into account as well as feelings Coping with conflict and 'negative' feelings Being more objective Challenging
J	Being organized Being decisive	Helping clients make decisions in a timely way (not prematurely) Being flexible
P	Being spontaneous Being flexible	Being organized (keeping to time and structure of session) Helping clients make decisions

Improving your skills

The main principle from MBTI theory for improving your counselling or coaching is to develop and confirm your own type's strengths first and then to work on the strengths of your non-preferences. The theory is also a useful counter to myths about 'the good counsellor' or 'the good coach': there are many ways of being effective in both professions.

Exercise 8.2

Apply Table 8.1 to your own counselling, coaching, etc. How well does your self-assessment or feedback from a colleague fit with MBTI theory? Ideally, ask for feedback from people of contrasting types to your own.

Core qualities

The term 'core qualities' or 'core conditions' is generally associated with person-centred counselling, but most approaches see the qualities of empathy, respect (warmth, acceptance) and genuineness as necessary, if not sufficient, for change in clients.

Empathy can be defined as the counsellor or coach communicating their understanding of their client's experiences to their client. MBTI theory suggests that it's very difficult to *really* empathize with someone of a different type to your own, especially if their dominant function and temperament are different. But the theory also suggests that genuine empathy becomes more likely as a result of knowing this limitation and knowing how profoundly different the types and temperaments are. One element here is that the obstacle of 'people are like me' should be less prominent or, alternatively, more conscious and therefore more readily countered, with the effect that empathy is likely to occur more quickly and more deeply.

For example, listening to an SJ client talk about pressure of work, I knew from temperament theory that responsibility was likely to be very prominent in her life and I used the word 'responsibility' with her. If I had not known (or guessed) that she was a developed SJ, and that

I am not an SJ, then I would either have taken longer to understand this quality in the client, or failed to appreciate it at all, or even have challenged it as an *intrinsically* unfulfilling way to be. That would have been deeply unempathic.

At the same time, some SJs are too responsible, and it affects their health and effectiveness. These SJs could usefully consider developing their P qualities but – according to temperament and type theory – they will always be basically responsible, and challenging the quality itself, rather than the overuse of it, is futile at best.

Similarly, MBTI theory is intended to encourage respect. A major aim is the constructive use of differences (Chapter 1), to counter the belief that 'people should be more like me'. Another, widely used term for respect in the counselling literature is 'acceptance'. MBTI theory implies that ESFPs will tend to be the most naturally accepting type, though they are not often found in counselling itself.

The third core quality, genuineness, is related to self-actualization, one of psychology's vaguest notions, but again MBTI theory offers a useful interpretation. First, it suggests some central characteristics of selves to be genuine or not genuine with. Second, it suggests that each type is genuine in different ways, e.g. Is in a more internal, more reflective way than Es, who are genuine in a more behavioural, visible way.

Listening

Exercise 8.3

Step 1   When you're listening well, what's going on in your mind? What does 'listening well' mean to you?

Step 2   Are there links between your observations and your type?

MBTI theory predicts that each type will have different strengths and weaknesses as a listener. As Table 8.1 implies, Ss (especially SPs?) may be more skilled at remembering exact words but more likely to miss underlying meanings and themes, while Ns (especially dominant INs?) may emphasize the skills of making links and assumptions so much that they miss most of the actual words, and therefore misunderstand. Similarly, Ts may focus too much or prematurely on theories and motives, Fs on emotions and values, Js on solutions and Ps on side issues.

The skill of paraphrasing is the key way of countering these and other obstacles to good listening. It could justifiably feature in all eight sets of 'aspects to work on' in Table 8.1, and it is the main way in which empathy is communicated. Paraphrasing is an artistic skill which can be defined as 'the attempt to restate, in a fresh way, the main part of what someone has said without adding any of your own ideas, feelings, interpretations, etc.' (Bayne *et al.*, 1999, p. 127). The primary aim of paraphrasing is to help your client clarify what they mean, feel and think but it also helps the person listening to check on how well they're listening.

If you're paraphrasing well, your client is more likely to say more and at a deeper level (or sometimes not to say anything, relieved to have been understood and accepted). If you're paraphrasing less well, your client is more likely to become disengaged or to try to paraphrase you!

MBTI theory is related to *how* we listen and communicate empathy. For example, in a qualitative study, Churchill and Bayne (2001) found marked contrasts between two ISTJ and two INFP counsellors in their replies to the question 'When you're actually with a client, how do you come to understand what's going on for your client?' One ISTJ replied:

> I take very little notice of the referral letter, I ask what's bothering the client. I listen and try to see what could be different, *are they looking at things ... might they be blinkered?* What are the issues likely to be? How receptive are they to me? I look for tension – that's usually reliable, the relevance of tensions to what they're recounting and where they are, and their resistances.

The other said:

> Well, first, what is the problem? I would ask for expansion and clarification – what's the cognition behind the problem? I look for patterns of behaviour, their emotional level because silly things can go out of proportion, *I look at their cognitions, and distortions in their cognitions, reading meanings into things which are not there.* I'm actively gathering information. I try to get into their core belief system: what does it mean to them? Where do their core beliefs come from: parents, their peer group?

The sections in italics show a similar concern to identify how the client's perceptions might be idiosyncratic.

The INFPs replied very differently. One INFP said:

> Well, the obvious things: if I've had a similar experience I can empathize. I try to enter into the situation, imagine what it must be like in my head; sometimes it moves me to tears; understanding; I imagine myself in it and what it must be like . . .

> Primarily through listening. Listen listen listen listen, to the story and the underneath, and to the feelings, which are then checked out, with the client, as tentatively as I can unless I'm really sure. A lot of reflection, I do a lot of empathy.

And the other:

> At the beginning of a process, you know, if it's a client I'm seeing for the first time or haven't seen very often, that's basically all I do, and some questions as open as they can be. I'm using less and less questions, actually, I have to say. With people that I've been working with for some time, I use a lot of immediacy, in that I know that that is my own particular style and that has evolved and I think immediacy is a very powerful tool and it brings into play the mutuality that Rogers talks about in the process.

Thus, the two ISTJ counsellors emphasized cognitions, and the two INFPs emotions. Another dramatic contrast is the way the INFPs described using their own emotional responses. For the ISTJs there was a drive to plan the therapy, define the problems, identify goals; for the INFPs it seems more important to fully enter the client's world. Moreover, although these counsellors have different theoretical approaches (the ISTJs were cognitive and psychodynamic respectively; the INFPs pure person-centred, and integrative on a psychodynamic foundation) what they had to say about counselling shows more commonality with someone of the same psychological type than someone with the same theoretical approach.

The next section discusses a contrasting aspect of counselling: whether or not there are links between type and choice of model.

Choice of counselling model(s)

Exercise 8.4

Step 1 Which counselling model or models are you most comfortable with?

Step 2 Can you say what factors were involved in your choice of this model or models?

Step 3 Do the relationships between type and choice of model, discussed next, suggest any possibilities for your own training as a counsellor or coach?

There is some evidence that psychological type is associated with choice of counselling model, most obviously that Ts tend to prefer cognitive models and Fs affective ones. Dodd and Bayne (in press) investigated type and choice of model in a sample of 123 experienced counsellors. We found far more NFs (55 per cent) than the UK norm of 14 per cent (Table 8.2), and relationships between the preferences, temperaments and types and more specific models, for example S, SJ and choice of cognitive behavioural therapy (CBT) (Table 8.3), N, FJ, INFJ and the psychoanalytic model (Table 8.4), and INFP and the psychosynthesis model (Table 8.5). The person-centred model, perhaps the most widely used in the UK and US (at least in theory), was not related to type

Table 8.2	**MBTI types (%s) of experienced counsellors (N = 123)**		
ISTJ	**ISFJ**	**INFJ**	**INTJ**
5	12	14	4
ISTP	**ISFP**	**INFP**	**INTP**
0	3	16	0
ESTP	**ESFP**	**ENFP**	**ENTP**
0	2	15	1
ESTJ	**ESFJ**	**ENFJ**	**ENTJ**
3	13	10	1

Source: Modified from Dodd and Bayne (in press)

Table 8.3	**Types (%s) of experienced CBT counsellors (N = 23)**		
ISTJ	ISFJ	INFJ	INTJ
13	22	0	9
ISTP	ISFP	INFP	INTP
0	4	9	0
ESTP	ESFP	ENFP	ENTP
0	0	4	0
ESTJ	ESFJ	ENFJ	ENTJ
9	26	4	0

Table 8.4	**Types (%s) or experienced psychoanalytic counsellors (N = 21)**		
ISTJ	ISFJ	INFJ	INTJ
5	10	38	0
ISTP	ISFP	INFP	INTP
0	0	10	0
ESTP	ESFP	ENFP	ENTP
0	0	14	0
ESTJ	ESFJ	ENFJ	ENTJ
0	14	10	0

Table 8.5	**Types (%s) of experienced psychosynthesis counsellors (N = 13)**		
ISTJ	ISFJ	INFJ	INTJ
0	0	15	0
ISTP	ISFP	INFP	INTP
0	0	54	0
ESTP	ESFP	ENFP	ENTP
0	0	23	0
ESTJ	ESFJ	ENFJ	ENTJ
0	8	0	0

(Table 8.6). Enthusiasts for the person-centred approach could interpret this as evidence for its superiority.

The relationships between type and choice of counselling model are consistent with MBTI theory. Thus SJs presumably tend to choose CBT

Table 8.6	**Types (%s) of experienced person-centred counsellors (N = 24)**

ISTJ	ISFJ	INFJ	INTJ
4	17	13	0
ISTP	**ISFP**	**INFP**	**INTP**
0	8	13	0
ESTP	**ESFP**	**ENFP**	**ENTP**
0	4	17	0
ESTJ	**ESFJ**	**ENFJ**	**ENTJ**
0	13	13	0

because of its structure and organization, and because it emphasizes replacing dysfunctional beliefs and attitudes with more realistic alternatives. Myers *et al.* (1998) described SJs' goals as 'to form a solid, substantial, and accurate understanding of the world and one's place in it' (p. 49), which seems a good description of part of the CBT approach. However, other types also find it comfortable and appealing: NTs, for example, are probably enjoying the rich variations in dysfunctional beliefs and replacing them with rational ones. Moreover, we found a substantial number of SJs in the person-centred counsellors (33 per cent) and psychoanalytic counsellors (24 per cent). Whether these SJs (nearly all SFJs) are more, or less, satisfied and effective in their work than SFJs working with the CBT model is an interesting question for future research.

INFJs were over-represented in the psychoanalytic counsellors. This psychological type uses its dominant N in developing and guiding people. When their types are well developed they like to 'Trust their inspirations and visions, using them to help others. Thrive on helping others resolve deep personal and ethical dilemmas' (Berens and Nardi, 1999, p. 38).

INFPs were strongly over-represented in the psychosynthesis counsellors, perhaps because INFPs tend to be particularly interested in 'contemplating life's mysteries ... in their search for wholeness' (Berens and Nardi, 1999, p. 42). Again, specific explanations of the link would be worth investigating.

Overall, the relationships between type and choice of counselling model suggest that experienced counsellors (the average age of our sample was early- to mid-50s, with twelve to thirteen years experience) tend to choose a model or models that fits them. However, as with other career choices (Chapter 3), this definitely does not mean that the 'wrong' type for a particular model should avoid it, rather that they should examine their choice and motives with particular care.

Choice of strategies and techniques

Some of the differences in clients' behaviour and experience related to MBTI theory are listed in Table 8.7. Making an attempt to assess a client's type will itself probably help counsellors and coaches to be less influenced by first impressions. Knowing that some clients will have opposite qualities to yourself can be very helpful. Moreover, knowing a clients' type or temperament (or current mode – Chapter 6) with reasonable accuracy allows you to adapt your own style if you wish.

For example, if you're an introvert counsellor or coach with an extravert client you might deliberately talk more than usual. Judy Provost (1993) thinks that counsellors can 'learn to "talk 16 types"' (p. 24). She adds that:

> Although counselors can build rapport by mirroring clients' types, this does not mean that counselors should or can 'become' the client's type. Counselors must be themselves and work from their own strengths. Talking a client's type is only the first step to reach a client.
>
> (p. 26)

Here Provost is discussing 'language' in the sense of behaviour as well as words, as in Table 8.7. According to type dynamics, counsellors and coaches should find clients whose fourth function is their (the counsellor's) dominant the most difficult.

The artistic element of counselling and coaching is very evident in 'talking a client's type' as it is in choosing when and how to support and when and how to challenge. Moreover, counsellors and coaches can usefully consider another strategy, that of discussing any differences with a client – for example, 'I wonder if you find me too quiet. Would you like me to speak more often or for us to try a role-play?' This is a standard strategy, a variation of the skill of immediacy (Bayne *et al.*, 1999), and MBTI theory adds greater clarity about some of the content.

Thus, the counsellor or coach might be more concrete and pragmatic with clients who prefer S (but also aware of their tendency to miss options); more experimental with Ns (but perhaps also helping them to focus); aware of the tendency of clients who prefer F to like to please

Table 8.7	**Psychological type and clients' probable behaviour in counselling and coaching**

Clients who prefer:	tend to:
Extraversion	– want more social chatter – want a more active counsellor – be less comfortable with reflection – be optimistic and energetic
Introversion	– be more at ease with silence – be less comfortable with action – be less enthusiastic about counselling
Sensing	– be concrete and detailed – go step by step – like a 'practical' approach – not see many options – be uncomfortable with novel techniques
Intuition	– give broad pictures – jump around from topic to topic – see unrealistic options – see lots of options – overlook facts – like novelty and imaginative approaches
Thinking	– avoid emotions, feelings and values in early sessions – need rationale and logic – be critical and sceptical – want to develop ways of measuring improvement – want to be admired – be competitive – want some professional distance
Feeling	– focus on values and networks of values – need to care (e.g. about a value, a person or an ideal) – be 'good clients' – want to be appreciated
Judging	– fear losing control – focus on outcome – find change stressful – need structure – need to achieve – work hard and tolerate discomfort
Perceiving	– avoid decisions – focus on process – need flexibility – avoid discomfort

Source: Modified from Bayne 1995 p. 112, developed from Miller (1991), Myers and McCaulley (1985) and Provost (1993)

and therefore to be too good a client (but also ready to challenge particularly gently, because Fs also tend to be more sensitive to criticism); ready *not* to press Ts on their emotions, especially early in counselling; more formal with Js (but also ready to challenge them to plan some 'play'); and more informal with Ps (but also ready to challenge them to plan a little more).

Another general strategy based on MBTI theory is to put more emphasis on clients' strengths than some approaches do. However, again there is a subtle variation. Sometimes a technique will be more effective when it *doesn't* appeal to a client's strength. This is because they've already tried that approach and it hasn't worked well or well enough. For example, cognitive approaches may (counter-intuitively) be most effective with clients who prefer F, or guided fantasies with clients who prefer S. I think the former idea is more likely than the latter but there's no good research on these possibilities yet. At the moment, it's a matter of using theory as a guide to sensitivity about whether, when and how to suggest a particular strategy or technique.

Choice of ways of presenting techniques

This choice for counsellors and coaches is part of the general strategy of matching or not matching the client. Here I think matching prevails. Thus it seems most likely to be effective when techniques and follow-ups are presented to Ss with the emphasis on attention to detail and in a step by step way, to Ns with a rationale and space for their creative input, to Ts logically and formally, and to Fs warmly. The principle is illustrated in Chapter 7 with reference to diets and exercise.

A good general principle is to suggest techniques as invitations to try something and see what happens. For example, two chair technique can seem a very odd thing to offer a client but less so when introduced as follows:

> There seem to be two parts of you arguing here, and going round and round, so you're feeling exhausted and hopeless ... I'd like to suggest an experiment to try and clarify the two sides. It means you sitting in this chair when you're arguing one way, and in this chair for the other side. Would that be ok?
>
> (Bayne *et al.*, 1999 p. 75)

Clients can then reject the suggestion more comfortably, or cope more readily with it not working, or, if it's 'homework', them not trying it at all.

The authentic chameleon issue

MBTI theory predicts that counsellors and coaches of some types will tend to be much more flexible than those of other types in their range of techniques and willingness (and ability) to match clients. At one end of a spectrum, we have counsellors who seem very consistent – Carl Rogers and Albert Ellis for example. Arnold Lazarus (in Dryden, 1991) criticized them for this, in Rogers' case for 'constantly offering his carefully cultivated warmth, genuineness and empathy to all his clients' (p. 18).

I think Lazarus is wrong about 'carefully cultivated' – Rogers seems a natural F (and Lazarus a natural ENTP) – but right in his view that clients want and need different styles of relationship. Lazarus is at the other end of this spectrum – comfortable in a variety of styles and with a wide range of techniques, and an enthusiastic proponent of matching. If he's an ENTP, he's an example of an authentic chameleon, because versatility is a characteristic quality of ENTPs and ENFPs. These two types tend to want to be and do everything. Other types prefer depth and specialisms to breadth and versatility. For all types, I think another positive implication of MBTI theory is that referral becomes more appealing and less, or not at all, like a failure on the part of counsellor, coach or client.

How much can people change?

Some aspects of people change as a result of counselling and some do not, or at least do so much less often and with much more effort. For example, the research on panic attacks and sexual problems (Seligman, 1995) and assertiveness training (Rakos, 1991) shows that positive changes are achieved often and quite quickly.

In contrast, other aspects of people such as sexual orientation and basic personality characteristics – like types and preferences (Bayne, 2004) and the Big Five factors (Miller, 1991) – change much less readily, if at all. This stability can be interpreted positively. First, it is part of having a sense of identity. Life would be very different if most people did not have stable identities and personalities. Second, it suggests that expectations of change through counselling and coaching need to be realistic.

For example, an introvert does not, at least not without a punitive amount of effort which continues to be punitive, change into an extravert. However, the introvert can usefully develop some extravert skills, just as extraverts can usefully develop introvert skills. Moreover, there is a special case in MBTI theory. When someone has lived as a psychological type other than their own, usually because of an extreme upbringing, they tend not to feel 'right' and can – though not always – change quickly and considerably in the direction of their true type (Bayne, 2004).

Another positive use of MBTI theory in relation to change in clients – if it's true – is that it counters pessimistic views about Ps. This is the equivalent of the prejudice against Ps in much of the job performance literature (Chapter 4). In counselling, Miller (1991) argued that clients who are low on Conscientiousness – Ps with little development of J in MBTI terms – are much less likely to change. He described one client as follows:

> A woman who has hated herself for years because she is overweight is encouraged to keep an eating diary and calculate her daily calorie intake. Despite continuing encouragement, she never buys a calorie counter and never records any of her meals. Her explanation is she is afraid she will be upset if she learns how much she really eats. We agree that it might be a good thing if she got upset about her eating habits. She continues to claim that low self-esteem due to obesity is her main problem, and she never complies with the plan (p. 430).

If this client really is unable to change, it's kinder not to persist, but MBTI theory suggests that the techniques tried were more likely to work for Js, and that other strategies would have been worth trying.

Conclusions

Counsellors, coaches and clients of different psychological types tend to be more comfortable with different stages, skills and aspects of counselling and coaching. MBTI theory makes empathy a more tangible idea, illustrates how difficult it is, provides a constructive framework for training and development, and explains relationships between the types and choices of counselling models. It also suggests realistic limits about those aspects of ourselves which we can change and those we can't.

9 Leading and managing

Definitions of 'leading' and 'managing' vary widely, with some writers using the two terms synonymously (e.g. Keirsey, 1998; Hogan and Hogan, 2001), and others seeing leading as one aspect of being a manager (e.g. Walck, 1996). David Keirsey (1998) argued that effective leaders understand the many forms of intelligence needed to achieve different organizational goals, and take their own form of intelligence and those of their staff into account. In his view, leaders have two main jobs: matching talents to tasks, and appreciation (pp. 287–8).

Matching talents to tasks was discussed in Chapter 3 (careers) and appreciation in Chapter 6 (in the sections on giving and receiving feedback and on assertiveness). Other sections and chapters particularly relevant to leading and managing are those on time (Chapter 5), communication (Chapter 6) and stress (part of Chapter 8). Effective communication is central to most approaches to being a good leader or manager, and is currently highlighted in ideas about 'emotional intelligence'. I see this as a useful term for selling an idea but think too much is claimed for it, both for its novelty and for its power. I return to 'emotional intelligence' in the next section.

In the rest of this chapter, I discuss an MBTI perspective on two general approaches to leading and managing: (1) the styles of leading proposed by Keirsey (1998), and (2) the 'dark side' of leadership (Hogan and Hogan, 2001). Then I focus in turn on four aspects of leading and managing:

1 Managing problems, including decision-making.
2 Goal-setting.
3 Managing money.
4 Managing change.

Styles of leading

The four styles of leading (and kinds of intelligence) proposed by Keirsey (1998) are tactical (associated with the SP temperament), logistical (SJ), diplomatic (NF) and strategic (NT). He sees them as complementary but suggests that leaders find it difficult to appreciate those forms of intelligence that aren't associated with their temperament and that they are therefore less likely to have developed.

The leadership style which each temperament is most likely to have developed, and the style which each is least likely to have developed, and therefore to appreciate (or even recognize) are as follows:

	Most developed	Least developed
SP Troubleshooters	Tactical	Diplomatic
SJ Stabilizers	Logistical	Strategic
NF Idealists	Diplomatic	Tactical
NT Rationals	Strategic	Logistical

Tactical leadership is about boldness and opportunism. 'Running through this style is a role of tactical utilitarianism – whatever needs to be done to solve a problem is done, and is done now' (Keirsey, 1998, p. 299). This troubleshooting style is based on a strong sense of reality and an ability to improvise. Everything is negotiable and the SP style is particularly valuable in crises. SPs 'can spur action in a leadership team as can no other type' (p. 301).

Other characteristics of tactical leaders follow, for example dislike of rules and routine and impatience with goal and mission statements. And so do their corresponding weaknesses: for example, rescuing a business is exciting, maintaining it is boring. Tactical leaders therefore need either to move on after resolving a crisis or to select developed SJs, NFs and NTs for their management team.

The main strengths and corresponding weaknesses, or relative weaknesses, of the four managerial/leadership styles suggested by Keirsey (1998) and Keirsey and Bates (1973) can be summarized as follows:

	Strengths	**Relative weaknesses**

Tactical (SP)	Trouble-shooting
	Practical
	Adaptable
	Appreciates others
	Risk-taking
	Detecting early signs of
	    trouble
		Theory
		Remembering earlier
		    decisions and
		    commitments
		Written documents
		The longer term

Logistical (SJ)	Stability
	Consolidating
	Rules, schedules,
	    procedures, policies,
	Routine
	Persistence
		Overemphasis on
		    means rather than ends
		Change
		Premature decisions
		Complexity
		Self-care
		Gloom
		Appreciating others

Diplomatic (NF)	Drawing out the
	    best in people (career
	    development, personal
	    growth)
	Appreciating others
	Idealism
	Aware of the 'climate'
	Public relations
		The organization's needs
		Self-care
		Structure
		Forgetting negative events
		Need for appreciation
		Wanting to please
		    everyone

Strategic (NT)	Vision Prototypes Scepticism Ingenuity Principles	Maintenance Crises Not stating what is obvious to them Appreciating others

Keirsey and Bates (1973) give a useful overview:

> Each style of leadership has its own unique contribution to make to the working situation. SJs lend stability and confidence. SPs make excellent problem-solvers and lend excitement. NTs provide vision and theoretical models for change. NFs lubricate the interpersonal fabric of an organization and can predict the social consequences of the NT's theoretical models.
>
> (pp. 152–3)

Emotional intelligence

Diplomatic (NF) managers and leaders seem most likely to be 'emotionally intelligent' in the broad sense of Daniel Goleman (1995) and others. A diplomatic style of leadership is most likely to be experienced as caring and inspiring. It may also be the most likely to reduce turnover.

For example, a survey of 200,000 employees found that 'employees leave managers, not companies' (Buckingham, 2000 p. 45), and that employees expect their managers (at all levels of management) to care about them as individuals. They also want to know what is expected of them, to have a role that fits their abilities, and to 'receive positive feedback and recognition regularly for work well done' (p. 45). Three of these four expectations are highly consistent with Keirsey's view of effective leadership, stated at the beginning of this chapter. What they neglect though is the leadership strengths for organizations of the Strategic, Logistical and Tactical styles.

Thus from an MBTI perspective, 'emotional intelligence' puts too much emphasis on one leadership style. There are other problems with the concept (and movement) too: first, that much, perhaps all of it, is not new – I see it as largely a repackaging of assertiveness theory in its humanistic form (Dickson, 1987; Bayne, 2000); second, that valid measurement has so far proved elusive (Davies *et al.*, 1998; cf. Caruso, 2001; Dulevicz and Higgs, 2001); third, that its significance has been exaggerated and that it's been oversimplified (Woodruffe, 2001; McCrae, 2001); and fourth, that the features of various conceptions of emotional intelligence map onto the five factor model of personality (McCrae, 2001).

This latter criticism is that emotional intelligence is just another way of describing the five basic personality factors (four of which, as discussed in Chapter 2, correlate highly with the MBTI preferences). Thus, Extraversion relates to the Optimism element of emotional intelligence, Openness (or SN) to Emotional self-awareness, Agreeableness (or TF) to Empathic awareness, and Conscientiousness (or JP) to Persistence. There are several implications of these relationships between personality characteristics and elements of emotional intelligence. First, such people (ENFJs) are rare. Second, the characteristics, by definition, are relatively stable, when the proponents of emotional intelligence tend to see them as malleable. Third, it's actually quite easy to measure emotional intelligence conceived in this way: just use the MBTI or, to include low Anxiety, the NEO-PI (McCrae, 2001).

Emotional intelligence has also been defined as a set of abilities. Robert McCrae suggests that measuring it with a battery of performance tests then becomes more appropriate. A parallel tension exists between measures of type and potential measures of type development (Bayne, 2004). Overall, 'emotional intelligence' seems to me a useful marketing term. It draws attention to valuable aspects of being a good manager but at the same time may contribute to neglecting other aspects.

Developing a style of leading

Keirsey argues that: 'It takes continuous practice to become highly proficient in doing anything, and continuous practice is done only by someone who is interested in and enjoys a particular kind of work' (pp. 293-4).

We know that thousands of subskills underly complex skills. Studies cited by Anderson (2000) show that there are something like 50 000 rules for playing chess, and that 'no one produced work reflecting genius until after 10 years of work in a particular field' (p. 324). Mozart *isn't* an exception, according to Anderson, because his first symphony, written when he was 8 years old, and his other early works, 'are not of a genius caliber' (p. 324).

High-level achievement therefore requires intensive practice and feedback as well as a natural predisposition. Fortunately, there is improvement meanwhile and it's possible to be sufficiently effective for most purposes without being a virtuoso, but it doesn't leave time, at least not for most people, to develop other skills to the same degree. Reasonable encouragement, or at least not drastic discouragement, may also play a part. However, Keirsey is more cautious in some of his statements about development than others. Thus, he sees each temperament as able to become 'fairly smart' (p. 298) at other forms of intelligence than their natural one – but his basic view is that if you want the best fit (virtuosity) and, I would add, greater well-being, then choose someone with the appropriate temperament for the particular task.

The main source on MBTI theory and developing leaders is Catherine Fitzgerald and Linda Kirby's (1997) book. It takes a very broad research-based approach to such topics as 360° feedback, FIRO-B, the

MBTI Step II, and development during organizational change and in management simulations. Surprisingly, it doesn't include Keirsey's ideas.

The 'dark side' of leadership

Hogan and Hogan's (2001) view of leadership (and management – they use the terms interchangeably) is in some respects the same as MBTI theory's and in others contrasts with it. They define leadership in a way which is broadly consistent with Keirsey's dual emphasis on matching talent and task and on appreciation, as 'the ability to build and maintain an effective team, one that can outperform its competition' (p. 40), but their focus is on the goal whereas Keirsey's is on the methods of achieving it.

Then they focus on leadership *incompetence* for three reasons. First, in their view it's easier to define undesirable qualities than desirable ones. By undesirable qualities, they mean for example, failure to delegate or prioritize, inability to maintain relationships, inability to build a team, poor judgement and having a 'personality disorder'. Second, these undesirable qualities are easier to study 'because there are so many bad managers in every organization' (p. 40). Third, they want to alleviate some of the suffering caused by bad managers.

They concentrate on the personality disorders. They see each disorder as coexisting with strong social skills, which means that they tend to be noticed only after a long period, and as compulsive. 'The person repeatedly engages in the same self-defeating behaviour' (p. 51). From an MBTI perspective, some particularly interesting features of their descriptions is that each disorder has some management strengths, each can be seen as in part an example of type development gone wrong, and that most of them also include a high level of anxiety.

For example, at their best, managers who have the disorder Hogan and Hogan call *excitable* tend to be enthusiastic about new projects and to be empathic, but at their worst they need a lot of reassurance, are easily disappointed, and when they're disappointed they tend to leave or withdraw. Similarly, at their best, managers who are *argumentative* tend to be thoughtful and perceptive but at their worst they expect to be cheated and betrayed, and they attack when they think this has happened. In MBTI terms these are not aspects of psychological type, at least not in normal development.

MBTI theory and the 'dark side' approach agree on the importance of personality, on goals, on seeing the issue as one of managerial development, and on the value of rigorously defined psychometric tests, but differ in emphasis in a way reminiscent of the two philosophies (Thinking and Feeling) of giving feedback discussed in Chapter 6. Thus, Hogan and Hogan seek to identify and challenge various kinds of incompetence and disorder, while also recognizing corresponding strengths, and the MBTI approach is to identify strengths and build on those, while also recognizing corresponding weaknesses. In practice, both approaches might well sound very similar at different stages of a development interview, but the difference in emphasis can be a vital one, as it can in giving feedback (Chapter 6).

Managing problems

MBTI theory implies the following model of problem-management. A perfect manager would be equally skilled at all the stages, but the theory says that this is very unlikely. Therefore, consistent with Keirsey's four styles of intelligence and leadership, there are no perfect managers but rather several different, complementary ways of being a good manager.

Stage 1 (Sensing): Define the problem or situation

> What are the facts?
> What has actually happened?
> What happened before in related situations?
> What resources are available?

Stage 2 (Intuition): Interpret it

> What other ways (however unlikely) are there to look at this?
> What are all the possible solutions, including absurd ones?
> Are any theories, models or frameworks relevant?

Stage 3 (Thinking): Analyse it

> Which is the logical solution?
> What are the pros and cons of each possible solution? Long- and short-term.
> What if no action is taken?

Stage 4 (Feeling): Evaluate it

What are the likely effects on you and other people? Long- and short-term.

What values is each possible solution consistent with or antagonistic to?

Variations of this model are in Hirsh and Kummerow (2000) and Myers with Kirby and Myers (1998).

According to type dynamics, each of us is most likely to neglect the stages in the model which correspond to our non-preferences. Neglecting a stage makes the following effects more likely:

Stage 1 (S)   There's an unforeseen practical difficulty.
You discover you should have checked your facts.
You ignored lessons from the past.

Stage 2 (N)   Another solution would have been much better.

Stage 3 (T)   There are unexpected and unpleasant consequences.

Stage 4 (F)   The solution turns out to be inconsistent with an important value.
The solution upsets you or others, to your surprise.

Conversely, MBTI theory suggests that one or two of the stages will be easy for each person (assuming sufficient type development). Moreover, it can be useful, and sometimes transforming, to consult someone of a different psychological type to your own, e.g. opposite dominant function, for their view of an issue or problem.

Exercise 9.1

Which stages in the problem-solving model are most comfortable for you? Which are least comfortable? Which are you most effective with? And which least?

Exercise 9.2

Do you compensate for your least effective strategy? Do you compensate enough? If not, how might you improve your use of this stage of the model?

Making decisions

Stages 3 and 4 of the problem-solving model are concerned with two ways of making decisions. One assumption, in the model and in MBTI theory, is that decisions made using *both* T and F, especially when they are reasonably developed, will tend to be better decisions. This explicit recognition of the value of F – and indirectly of emotions as vital clues to F values – is a valuable feature of 'Emotional Intelligence' too. As Goleman (1995) rather poetically put it, our emotions 'have a mind of their own, one which can hold views quite independent of our rational mind' (p. 20).

A second assumption from MBTI theory is that each of us should give most weight to our own preference, either T or F, when finally making a decision. Thus, strictly, the sequence of the model is S, N, F, T for Thinking types and S, N, T, F for Feeling types. Type dynamics could add further variations but, as the model is fluid rather than linear, this would probably not be a helpful complexity.

Goal-setting

The following checklist, from Kroeger with Thuesen (1992, p. 65), is intended to make achieving good organizational goals more likely. Underlying it is, of course, a main strength of each preference.

- Did everyone get a chance to speak about the goals?
- Has there been ample time to reflect on the goals?
- Are the goals realistic?
- Do the goals allow for future expansion?
- Are the goals consistent with the organizational mission?
- Will everyone in the organization commit to the goals?
- Is there a plan to monitor progress towards reaching the goals?
- Do the goals allow for emergencies and the unexpected?

Otto Kroeger and Janet Thuesen also discuss *how* people with different preferences approach goal-setting, some of the problems that can arise, and strategies to try. Taking E and I first, Es tend to talk, and also to assume that 'silence equals consent'. Introverts can therefore be torn between wanting to reflect in silence and perhaps at length, and speaking up uncomfortably. Moreover, Es tend, as do some Is, to speak to clarify their thinking and therefore with no commitment to what they say at that point: 'I'm just thinking out loud.' Is may misinterpret these thoughts as decisions.

The strategies for trying to reduce misunderstandings are obvious. For example, allowing time for both talking and reflection, remembering that silence doesn't always mean consent, being assertively clear and direct – 'I'd like more time to think about this', 'I'm thinking out loud', 'Off the top of my head'. The underlying principles here are knowing and respecting both yourself and those with different preferences. A further strategy is to use your non-preferences some of the time, e.g. an Introvert taking the risk of speaking spontaneously.

Similarly, Ss tend to like and need specific, attainable, practical goals while Ns tend to like and need inspiring, general goals. Each can have trouble with the other's idea of a goal: seeing it as banal and obvious on the one hand or ridiculous and futile on the other. Again, the strategy is to respect difference. Ss can value Ns speculating and dreaming for a while – there might be something useful in there – and Ns can value Ss realism and practicality – the goal is more likely to be achieved. This can result in avoiding conflict and stalemates, and in better goals.

Ts and Fs become committed to a goal in very different ways. Ts tend to want a goal to be 'state of the art', objectively good, and to believe that 'I don't have to like you to work with you.' Conversely, Fs tend to want a goal to have good effects on people, and to believe that harmony in a group is important. MBTI theory implies that Ts can try to accept that feeling good at work matters and to realize that goals that alienate people may not be worthwhile, and that Fs can try to value disagreements and to accept that sometimes everyone doesn't feel good about a goal or decision. Kroeger and Thuesen suggest that Ts can try saying 'How will this goal affect the people who must carry it out?', and Fs 'This goal makes sense on the bottom line, and therefore personal differences should be set aside' (1992, p. 84).

Exercise 9.3

Take a current goal in your organization and try saying about it, to yourself, the two sentences Kroeger and Thuesen suggest above. Observe your reactions carefully and write them down.

Finally, Js press for closure and then follow through, while Ps keep things open – for Ps, goals are 'always emerging' (p. 77). On the one hand, goals are solid, but may need reassessing from time to time; on the other, they're guidelines, and always open to change. Kroeger and Thuesen suggest that the best goals will be set when Js allow time for discussing several options and Ps settle on something and stay with it for a while.

A useful general principle, in goal-setting and generally, is that 'strengths maximized can become liabilities' (Kroeger and Thuesen, 1992, p. 85) or, as Kroeger and Thuesen put it in an earlier book: 'Too much of a good thing is a bad thing' (1988, p. 98). The strategy that follows from this principle is to remember our non-preferences and include them. Thus, if your team, department or organization is biased towards some of the psychological types (which it probably is), this means deliberately seeking out minority views and considering them seriously. For example, an ENFJ manager knows that his analytic thinking skills are relatively weak so he asks people with highly developed T, and who he trusts, to observe him in meetings and give him their views later.

Managing money

Exercise 9.4

Step 1   Describe your attitude to money and how you spend it, e.g. if you have control or influence over a budget

Step 2   Compare your attitudes and behaviour with the tendencies for your type ssummarized below.

Step 3a   If your attitudes and behaviour are not consistent with your type, did your upbringing have a strong effect on you where money is concerned?

Step 3b   If they are consistent, does this comparison suggest any ways in which you might usefully add to or modify your approach to spending it?

MBTI theory assumes that each type has a natural approach to money, derived from core motives. Knowing your own approach can help you to use it most effectively, probably by moderating it and supplementing it with aspects of other approaches.

Taking a simple level of the theory, SPs (a combination of Sensing and Perceiving) tend to spend money to feel free and excited; SJs tend to be careful with money, to try to achieve security and stability; NTs try to spend it perfectly (because competence is their core motive); and NFs tend to ignore it (because their core motive is rather more vague and not materialistic, i.e. 'self-actualization').

In the theory each of the natural approaches is valid and has strengths (Linder, 2000a, b). However, the strengths can be taken too far and they can be modified as part of type development. For example, an SP might find excitement from other sources than spending money and, through developing their Judging 'side', might build up some savings. Similarly, NTs, especially INTPs, might set a time limit on their detailed comparative analyses of a particular purchase, and develop their ability to make decisions in an F way to supplement (not replace or equal) their T decisions.

One complication is that early life experience can confuse the predicted relationships between temperament and money, for example an NF trying to behave like her NT mother. While this seems a realistic complication, it does, of course, make applying the ideas more difficult.

At the level of behaviour, Ray Linder (2000b) finds the following tendencies for each dominant function:

IS   Plan and save. Strong loyalty to stores and brands.

ES   Saving is impractical. Buy it *now*.

IN   Spend elegantly and tastefully. 'The ideal is more important than the cost.' 'Insightful gift givers.' (p. 5)

EN   'Natural savers.' (p. 4)

IT   'Highly analytical comparison shoppers' who are concerned with the intrinsic value – the right price – of something.

ET   The most organized approach: records, receipts, etc.

IF   'Of all types, money matters least.' (p. 6)

EF   Use money to care for others.

Managing change

Several factors are making change in organizations more common, including the global economy, new technology and political forces. Practices like 'delayering' which either enrich jobs previously at a lower level or ask for more responsibility for the same pay, depending on your point of view, also mean change. At the same time, more participative management styles are more appropriate for a more educated workforce, and therefore managers need to sell change rather than impose it. The Diplomatic style of leadership may generally be the most effective in this situation.

MBTI theory implies the following individual differences in response to a proposed change:

- Extraverts will probably want to discuss the change with several people; introverts to reflect on it alone or with one other person.
- Ss will probably want a specific, practical justification, and a step-by-step implementation; Ns a broad, inspiring rationale and a quick radical adoption.
- Ts will probably be objective and analytical, and focused on the task and its effect on the efficiency; organization of the Fs more concerned about the effects on people.
- Js will probably want a schedule and closure; Ps to keep their options open.

NPs and SJs are the two most opposed types on change: NPs searching for new possibilities, more likely to be bored by continuity and very open to change (but tending to resist closure and completion), SJs seeking closure and stability, less happy with risk (but tending to resist new options, 'change for the sake of it', and re-thinks). At best, there is a creative tension and mutual respect between these two types.

A central theme of MBTI theory is evident in the list above: that the best results in managing change will probably draw on the strengths of all the types. The list also suggests ways of presenting the change and probable kinds of objection to it. Because the leaders of organizations tend to be Ns and often TJs as well, the main dangers are neglecting team spirit, morale and emotions, including feelings of loss, when it is people who have to make any change work, and secondly, going too fast, when it takes time to listen and to respond to reactions and ideas. Type can therefore help people understand both their own reactions to proposed change and the reactions of others with radically different psychological types. Nancy Barger and Linda Kirby's (1995) book is a detailed review of MBTI theory and planning, implementing and managing change in organizations.

Conclusions

Good managers and leaders can be seen as having two main jobs: matching talents to tasks, and appreciation. Four complementary leadership styles – tactical, logistical, diplomatic and strategic – each have strengths and corresponding weaknesses. 'Emotional intelligence' is central to only one of the styles.

The 'dark side' and MBTI approaches to leadership may differ mainly in emphasis, but it's an important difference. Models of problem-management and goal-setting based on MBTI theory use the strengths of all the preferences. Knowing your type's motives for spending money and characteristic ways of spending it may help you to spend it more effectively. Similarly, MBTI theory suggests ways of planning, implementing and managing organizational change which take into account the core motives and strengths of all the psychological types.

MBTI Resources

1 The internet

One of the best of the hundreds of MBTI sites is:

www.personalitytype.com which has brief profiles of each type, with sections on observing, loving and parenting each type, communicating and career choices.

Three others, each with a links section for easy transfer to other MBTI sites, are: *www.typetalk.com* which is Otto Kroeger's site, *Smyers@teamtechnology.co.uk* and *www.aptcentral.org*

2 Membership organizations

BAPT (British Association for Psychological Type)
PO Box 404
Norwich, MLO
NR2 3WB
Phone: 01603 446963
e-mail: *admin@bapt.org.uk*

APT (Association for Psychological Type)
Website: *www.aptcentral.org*

3 Research

CAPT (Center for Applications of Psychological Type)
Phone: 001 800 777 2278

e-mail: *capt@capt.org*
Website: *www.capt.org*

Online bibliography (7,000 + items) of type research. Supplies MBTI books and runs MBTI training in the USA.
001 800 777 2278

4 Training in the UK

You need to be officially qualified to use the MBTI itself, either as a chartered psychologist or (more ethically) through specific training. OPP is the licensing body for the whole of Europe.

Phone: 01865 404500
Website: *www.opp.co.uk.*

References

Allen, J. and Brock, S. A. (2000) *Health Care Communication and Personality Type*. London: Routledge.

Anderson, J. (2000) *Learning and Memory: An Integrated Approach*. Chichester: Wiley, 2nd edn.

Anderson, N. and Cunningham-Snell, N. (2000) Perspectives on selection. In N. Chmiel (ed.) *Introduction to Work and Organizational Psychology*. Oxford: Blackwell.

Anderson, N., Herriot, P. and Hodgkinson, G. P. (2001) The practitioner–researcher divide in industrial, work and organizational (IWO) psychology: where are we now and where do we go from here? *Journal of Occupational and Organizational Psychology 74*, 391–412.

Barger, N. and Kirby, L. (1995) *The Challenge of Change in Organizations*. Palo Alto, CA: Davies and Black.

Barrick, M. R. and Mount, M. K. (1991) The big five personality dimensions and job performance: a meta-analysis. *Personnel Psychology 44*, 1–26.

Bayne, R. (1995) *The Myers-Briggs Type Indicator. A Critical Review and Practical Guide*. Cheltenham: Nelson Thornes.

Bayne, R. (2000) Assertiveness. In C. Feltham and I. Horton (eds). *Handbook of Counselling and Psychotherapy*. London: Sage

Bayne, R. (2004) *Ideas and Evidence: Critical Reflections on MBTI Theory and Practice*. Gainesville, FL: CAPT

Bayne, R., Horton, I., Merry, T., Noyes, E. and McMahon, G. (1999) *The Counsellor's Handbook*. Cheltenham: Nelson Thornes, 2nd edn.

Bayne, R. and Kwiatkowski, R. (1998) Type and time orientation: a partial replication and critique of Harrison and Lawrence. *Journal of Psychological Type 47*, 28–34.

Bayne, R., Merry, T. and McMahon, G. (2003) Counselling. In R. Bayne and I. Horton (eds). *Applied Psychology*. London: Sage.

Bayne, R. and O'Neill, F. (1988) Handwriting and personality: an empirical test of expert graphologists' judgements. *Guidance and Assessment Review 4*, 1–3.

Berens, L. V. (1999) *Dynamics of Personality Type. Understanding and Applying Jung's Cognitive Processes.* Huntingdon Beach, CA: Telos Publications.

Berens, L. V. (2000) *Understanding Yourself and Others. An Introduction to Temperament.* Huntingdon Beach, CA: Telos Publications.

Berens, L. V. and Nardi, D. (1999) *The Sixteen Personality Types, Descriptions for Self-Discovery.* Huntingdon Beach, CA: Telos Publications.

Bimrose, J., Mulvey, M. R. and La Gro, N. (2003) Careers guidance. In R. Bayne and I. Horton (eds). *Applied Psychology.* London: Sage.

Blackman, M. C. and Funder, D. C. (2002) Effective interview practices for accurately assessing counterproductive traits. *International Journal of Selection and Assessment 10*, 109–16.

Boice, R. (1994) *How Writers Journey to Comfort and Fluency.* London: Praeger.

Bond, M. (1986) *Stress and Self-Awareness: A Guide for Nurses.* London: Heinemann.

Boniwell, I. and Zimbardo, P. (2003) Time to find the right balance. *The Psychologist 16*, 129–31.

Bridges, W. (1992) *The Character of Organizations.* Palo Alto, CA: CPP.

Briner, R. (2000) Evidence-based human resource management. In L. Trinder, with S. Reynolds (eds) *Evidence-Based Practice: A Critical Appraisal.* Oxford: Blackwell.

Brock, S. A. (1994) *Using Type in Selling.* Palo Alto, CA: CPP.

Brownell, K. D. and Rodin, J. (1994) The dieting maelstrom. Is it possible and advisable to lose weight? *American Psychologist 49*, 801–10.

Brue, S. (2003) The intuitive function and physical exercise. *Bulletin of Psychological Type*, spring, 57–60.

Buckingham, G. (2000) Same difference. *People Management* February, 44–6.

Buckingham, M. (2001) What a waste. *People Management* October, 36–40.

Buyssen, H. (1996) *Traumatic Experiences of Nurses: When your Profession Becomes a Nightmare.* London: Jessica Kingsley.

Carr, S. (1997) *Type Clarification: Finding the Fit.* Oxford: OPP.

Carskadon, T. (2002) *Journal of Psychological Type:* A 25-year history. *Journal of Psychological Type 61*, 3–37.

Cartwright, S. and Cooper, C. L. (1996) Public policy and occupational health psychology in Europe. *Journal of Occupational Health Psychology 1*, 349–61.

Caruso, D. (2001) Reply to Woodruffe. *People Management* April, 40–1.

Churchill, S. and Bayne, R. (1998) Psychological type and conceptions of empathy in experienced counsellors. *Counselling Psychology Quarterly 11*, 379–90.

Churchill S. and Bayne, R. (2001) Psychological type and conceptions of empathy in experienced counsellors: qualitative results. *Counselling Psychology Quarterly 14*, 203–17

Clack, G. S. (submitted for publication) The relationship of psychological type in UK doctors to medical speciality choice and job satisfaction.

Cockerill, I. M. and Riddington, M. E. (1996) Exercise dependence and associated disorders: a review. *Counselling Psychology Quarterly 9*, 119–29.

Cohen, S., Frank, E., Doyle, W. J., Skoner, D. P., Rabin, B. S. and Gwaltney, J. M. (1998) Types of stressors that increase susceptibility to the common cold in healthy adults. *Health Psychology 17, 3*, 214–23. Cockerill, I. M. and Riddington, M. E. (1996) Exercise dependence and associated disorders: a review. *Counselling Psychology Quarterly 9*, 119–29.

Cooper, C. L., Dewe, P. J. and O'Driscoll, M. P. (2001) *Organizational Stress. A Review and Critique of Theory, Research and Applications.* London: Sage.

Costa, P. T. and McCrae, R. R. (1992a) Four ways five factors are basic. *Personality and Individual Differences 13*, 653–65.

Costa, P. T. and McCrae, R. R. (1992b) *The NEO PI-R Professional Manual.* Odessa, FL: Psychological Assessment Resources.

Costa, P. T., McCrae, R. R. and Kay, G. G. (1995) Persons, places and personality: career assessment using the revised NEO personality inventory. *Journal of Career Assessment 3*, 123–39.

Davies, M., Stankow, L. and Roberts, R. D. (1998) Emotional intelligence: in search of an elusive construct. *Journal of Personality and Social Psychology 75*, 989–1015.

Dean, G. (1986–7) Does astrology need to be true? *The Skeptical Inquirer 11*, 166–83, 257–73.

Demarest, L. (1997) *Looking at Type in the Workplace.* Gainesville, FL: CAPT.

Dewitte, S. and Lens, W. (2000) Procrastinators lack a broad action prospective. *European Journal of Personality 14*, 121–40.

Dickson, A. (1987) *A Woman in Your Own Right.* London: Quartet.

DiTiberio, J. K. and Hammer, A. L. (1993) *Introduction to Type in College.* Palo Alto, CA: CPP.

DiTiberio, J. K. and Jensen, G. H. (1995) *Writing and Personality.* Palo Alto, CA: Davies-Black.

Dodd, N. and Bayne, R. (in press) Psychological type and choice of counselling model by experienced counsellors. *Journal of Psychological Type.*

Dodd, N. and Bayne, R. (submitted for publication). Internal reliability and item analysis of the Keirsey Temperament Sorter II.

Doyle, C. E. (2003) *Work and Organizational Psychology: An Introduction with Attitude.* Hove: Psychology Press.

Dryden, W. (1991) *A Dialogue with Arnold Lazarus. 'It depends'.* Milton Keynes: OU Press.

Duan, C. and Hill, C. E. (1996) The current state of empathy research. *Journal of Counselling Psychology 11*, 379–90.

Dulevicz, V. and Higgs, M. (2001) Reply to Woodruffe. *People Management* April, 41–2.

Dunning, D. (2003) *Introduction to Type and Communication.* Palo Alto, CA: CPP.

Egan, G. (2002) *The Skilled Helper*. London: Thomson, 7th edn.

Elbow, P. (1997) Freewriting and the problem: wheat and tares. In J. M. Moxley and T. Taylor (eds) *Writing and Publishing for Academic Authors*. London: Bowman and Littlefield, 2nd edn.

Fitzgerald, C. and Kirby, L. K. (1997) (eds) *Developing Leaders: Research and Application in Psychological Type and Leadership Development*. Palo Alto, CA: Davies-Black.

Fitzsimmons, S. (1999) *Type and Time Management*. Edmonton: Psychometrics Canada Ltd.

Fleck, D. and Bayne, R, (1990) Psychological type and the design of application forms. *Guidance and Assessment Review 6*, 2–4.

Funder, D. C. (1995) On the accuracy of personality judgment: a realistic approach. *Psychological Review 102*, 652–70.

Furnham, A. (1996) The big five versus the big four: the relationship between the Myers-Briggs Type Indicator (MBTI) and NEO-PI five factor model of personality. *Personality and Individual Differences 21*, 303–7.

Furnham, A. and Heaven, P. (1999) *Personality and Social Behaviour*. London: Arnold.

Goleman, D. (1995) *Emotional Intelligence*. New York: Bantam Books.

Hai, D. M., Rossi, J. and Ziemelis, A. (1986) Personality types: comparison of job applications and applicants. *Psychological Reports 59*, 1119–25.

Hammer, A. L. (ed.) (1996) *MBTI Applications, A Decade of Research on the Myers-Briggs Type Indicator*. Palo Alto, CA: CPP.

Hammer, A. L. and Huszczo, G. E. (1996) Teams. In A. L. Hammer (ed). *MBTI Application. A Decade of Research on the Myers-Briggs Type Indicator*. Palo Alto, CA: CPP.

Hammer, A. L. and Macdaid, G. P. (1992) *Career Report Manual*. Palo Alto, CA: CPP.

Harrison, D. and Lawrence, G. (1985) Psychological type and time orientation: do middle school students differ in projecting their personal futures? *Journal of Psychological Type 9*, 10–15.

Heinrich, K. T. and Pfeiffer, C. A. (1989). Using the MBTI to personalize the teaching of interviewing skills. *Proceedings of the Eight Biennial International Conference of the Association for Psychological Type*. University of Colorado, Boulder pp. 77–81. Kansas City, Missouri: Association for Psychological Type.

Herriot, P. and Pemberton, C. (1995) *New Deals*. Chichester: Wiley

Herriot, P. and Wingrove, J. (1984) Decision processes in graduate preselection. *Journal of Occupational Psychology 57*, 269–76.

Hill, C. E. and O'Brien, K. M. (1999) *Helping Skills: Facilitating Exploration, Insight and Action*. Washington, DC: APA.

Hirsh, S. K. and Kummerow, J. M. (2000) *Introduction to Type in Organizations*. Oxford: OPP, 3rd edn.

Hogan, R. and Hogan, J. (2001) Assessing leadership: a view from the dark side. *International Journal of Selection and Assessment 9*, 40–51.

Holland, J. L. (1996) Exploring careers with a typology: what we have learned and some new directions. *American Psychologist 51*, 397–406.

Hubble, M. A., Duncan, B. I. and Miller, S. D. (1999) (eds) *The Heart and Soul of Change: What Works in Therapy?* Washington, DC: APA

Hutton, W. (2003) In pursuit of true happiness. *The Observer, 9 March*, 30.

Jensen, G. H. (1987) Learning styles. In J. A. Provost and S. Anchors (eds) *Applications of the Myers-Briggs Type Indicator in Higher Education*. Palo Alto, CA: CPP.

Jones, F. and Bright, J. (2001) *Stress: Myth, Theory and Research*. London: Prentice-Hall.

Joseph, J. (2003) *The Gene Illusion. Genetic Research in Psychiatry and Psychology Under the Microscope*. Ross-on-Wye: PCCS Books.

Judge, T. A., Higgins, C. A., Thoresen, C. J. and Barrick, M. A. (1999) The Big Five personality traits, general mental ability, and career success across the life span. *Personnel Psychology 52*, 621–52.

Jung, C. G. (1923) *Psychological Types*. London: Routledge.

Keirsey, D. (1998) *Please Understand Me II*. Del Mar, CA: Prometheus Nemesis.

Keirsey, D. and Bates, M. (1973) *Please Understand Me*, Del Mar, CA: Prometheus Nemesis, 3rd edn.

Kelly, E. J. (1985) Chessmaster personality and type: comparative analyses with average players and non-players. *Journal of Psychological Type 9*, 41–9.

Kendall, E. (1998) *Myers-Briggs Type Indicator: European English Edition*. Manual Supplement. Oxford: OPP.

Kenrick, D. and Funder, D. C. (1988) Profiting from controversy: lessons from the person–situation debate. *American Psychologist 43*, 1, 23–34.

Klein, R. (1997) *Eat Fat*. London: Picador.

Kristof, A. L. (1996) Person–organisation fit: an integrative review of its conceptualisations, measurement, and implications. *Personnel Psychology 49*, 1–49.

Kroeger, O. (1985) Fat is a typological issue. *The Type Reporter 1*, 16–17.

Kroeger, O. and Thuesen, J. M. (1988) *Type Talk*. New York: Delacorte Press.

Kroeger, O., with Thuesen, J. M. (1992) *Type Talk at Work*. New York: Delacorte Press.

Kummerow, J. M. (1998) Uses of type in career counselling. In Myers, I. B. *et al. MBTI Manual*. Palo Alto, CA: CPP, 3rd edn.

Kummerow, J. M. (2001) Examining type bias and inclusivity: lessons from ethnic identity viewpoints. *Journal of Psychological Type 56*, 6–9.

Kummerow, J. M., Barger, N. J. and Kirby, L. K. (1997) *WorkTypes*. New York: Warner Books.

Kummerow, J. M. and McAllister, L. W. (1998) Team-building with the Myers-Briggs Type Indicator: case-studies. *Journal of Psychological Type 15*, 26–32.

Kummerow, J. M. and Quenk, N. L. (2003) *Understanding Your MBTI Step II Results.* Palo Alto, CA: CPP.

Kwiatkowski, R. and Hogan, D. (1999) Group membership. In R. Bayne, P. Nicolson and I. Horton (eds) *Counselling and Communication Skills for Medical and Health Practitioners.* Oxford: Blackwell.

Lawrence, G. D. (1993) *People Types and Tiger Stripes.* Gainesville, FL: CAPT. 3rd edn.

Lawrence, G. D. (1997) *Looking at Type and Learning Styles.* Gainesville, FL: CAPT.

Lawrence, G. D. (1998) *Descriptions of the Sixteen Types.* Gainesville, FL: CAPT.

Lawrence, G. D. and Martin, C. R. (2001) *Building People, Building Programs.* Gainesville, FL: CAPT.

Le Blanc, P., de Jonge, J. and Schaufeli, W. (2000) Job stress and health. In N. Chmiel (ed.) *Introduction to Work and Organizational Psychology.* Oxford: Blackwell.

Leonard, D. and Straus, S. (1997) Putting your company's whole brain to work. *Harvard Business Review* July–August, 111–21.

Lewis, C. (1992) *Employee Selection.* London: Hutchinson 2nd edn.

Linder, R. (2000a) *What Will I Do With My Money?: How your Personality Affects your Financial Behaviour.* Chicago: Northfield.

Linder, R. (2000b) Which way to the good life? *Bulletin of Psychological Type 23*, 4–6.

Loehlin, C. *et al.* (1998) Heritabilities of common and measure-specific components of the Big Five personality factors. *Journal of Research in Personality 32*, 431–53.

Loomis, A. B. (1999) *Write From the Start.* Gainesville, FL: CAPT.

McAdams, D. P. (1995) What do we know when we know a person? *Journal of Personality 63*, 365–96.

McCaulley, M. H. and Martin, C. R. (1995) Career assessment and the Myers-Briggs Type Indicator. *Journal of Career Assessment 3*, 219–39.

McCrae, R. R. (2001) Emotional intelligence from the perspective of the five-factor model of personality. In R. Bar-on and J. D. A. Barker (eds) *The Handbook of Emotional Intelligence.* San Francisco: Jossey-Bass.

McCrae, R. R. and Costa, P. T. (1989) Re-interpreting the Myers-Briggs Type Indicator from the perspective of the five factor model of personality. *Journal of Personality 57*, 17–37.

McDaniel, M. A., Whetzel, D. L., Schmidt, F. L. and Maurer, S. (1994). The validity of employment interviews: A comprehensive review and metanalysis. *Journal of Applied Psychology 79*, 599–616.

McGregor, D. (1960) *The Human Side of Enterprise.* New York: McGraw Hill.

McKenzie, R. (1983) *Treat Your Own Neck.* Waikanae, NZ: Spinal Publications.

McKenzie, R. (1988) *Treat Your Own Neck.* Waikanae, NZ: Spinal Publications.

McLeod, J. (2003) *An Introduction to Counselling*. Buckingham: OU Press, 3rd edn. Mann, H., Siegler, M. and Osmond, H. (1968) The many worlds of time. *Journal of Analytical Psychology 13*, 33–56.

Mann, H., Siegler, M. and Osmond, H. (1968) The many worlds of time. *Journal of Analytical Psychology 13*, 33–56.

Martin, C. R. (1995) *Looking at Type and Careers*. Gainesville, FL: CAPT.

Martin, C. R. (2003) *Quick Guide to the 16 Personality Types and Careers Mastery*. Huntingdon Beach, CA: Telos Publications.

Matthews, B. P. and Rodman, T. (1998) Managerial recruitment advertisements – just how market orientated are they? *International Journal of Selection and Assessment 6*, 240-8.

Miller, T. R. (1991) The psychotherapeutic utility of the five-factor model of personality: a clinician's experience. *Journal of Personality Assessment, 57* 415–33.

Mitroff, I. I. and Kilmann, R. H. (1975) Stories managers tell: a new tool for organizational problem-solving. *Management Review*, July, 18–28.

Morehouse, L. E. and Gross, L. (1977) *Total Fitness in 30 Minutes a Week*. St. Albans: Mayflower.

Mount, M. K. and Barrick, M. R. (1998) Five reasons why the 'Big Five' article has been frequently cited. *Personnel Psychology 51*, 849–57.

Myers, I. B. (1977) Making the most of individual differences in a changing society. *MBTI News 2*, 1–4.

Myers, I. B., with Kirby, L. K. and Myers, K. D. (1998) *Introduction to Type*. Oxford: Oxford Psychologists Press, 6th edn.

Myers, I. B. and McCaulley, M. H. (1985) *Manual: A Guide to the Development and Use of the Myers-Briggs Type Indicator*. Palo Alto, CA: CPP, 2nd edn.

Myers, I. B., with Myers, P. B. (1980) *Gifts Differing*. Palo Alto, CA: CPP.

Myers, I. B., McCaulley, M. H., Quenk, N. L. and Hammer, A. L. (1998) *Manual: A Guide to the Development and Use of the Myers-Briggs Type Indicator*. Palo Alto, CA: CPP, 3rd edn.

Myers, K. D. and Kirby, L. K. (1994) *Introduction to Type Dynamics and Type Development*. Palo Alto, CA: CPP.

Nardi, D. (1999) *Character and Personality Type. Discovering Your Uniqueness for Career and Relationship Success*. Huntingdon Beach, CA: Telos Publications.

O'Driscoll, M. and Cooper, C. L. (1996) Sources and management of excessive job stress and burnout. In P. Warr (ed.) *Psychology at Work*, Harmondsworth: Penguin, 4th edn.

Orlans, V. (2003) Counselling psychology in the workplace. In R. Woolfe, W. Dryden and S. Strawbridge (eds). *Handbook of Counselling Psychology*. London: Sage, 2nd edn.

Pennebaker, J. W., Colder, M. and Sharp, L. K. (1990) Accelerating the coping process. *Journal of Personality and Social Psychology 58*, 528–37.

Penner, R. (1992) Applying type in adapting to chronic illness. *Bulletin of Psychological Type 15*, 15–16.

Pinker, S. (2002) *The Blank Slate*. London: Allen Lane.

Plomin, R. (2001) Genetics and behaviour. *The Psychologist 14*, 134–39.

Premack, S. L. and Wanous, J. P. (1985) A meta-analysis of realistic job preview experiments. *Journal of Applied Psychology 70*, 706–19.

Price, R. E. and Patterson, F. (2003) Online application forms: psychological impact on applicants and implications for recruiters. *Selection and Development Review 19*, 12–19.

Provost, J. A. (1993) *Applications of the Myers-Briggs Type Indicator in Counseling: A Casebook*. Gainesville, FL: CAPT, 2nd edn.

Provost, J. A. (1998) *Procrastination*. Palo Alto, CA: CAPT, 3rd edn.

Quenk, N. L. (1993) *Beside Ourselves. Our Hidden Personality in Everyday Life*. Palo Alto, CA: CPP.

Quenk, N. L. (2002) *Was That Really Me?* Palo, Alto, CA: Davies-Black.

Quenk, N. L., Hammer, A. L. and Majors, M. (2001) *MBTI Step II Manual*. Palo Alto, CA: CPP.

Rakos, R. (1991) *Assertive Behaviour: Theory, Research and Training*. London: Routledge.

Rauch, J. (2003) Caring for your introvert. *The Atlantic Monthly 291*, 133–4 (*www.theatlantic.com*).

Robertson, I. J., Baron, H., Gibbons, P., MacIver, R. and Nyfield, G. (2000) Conscientiousness and managerial performance. *Journal of Occupational and Organizational Psychology 73*, 171–80.

Robertson, I. T. and Smith, M. (2001) Personnel selection. *Journal of Occupational and Organizational Psychology 74*, 441–72.

Robson, C. (2002) *Real World Research*. Oxford: Blackwell, 2nd edn.

Rogers, J. (1997) *Influencing Others Using the Sixteen Personality Types*. Cambridge: Management Futures Ltd.

Rosenthal, T. (1993) To soothe the savage breast. *Behaviour Research and Therapy, 31 5*, 439–62.

Rowland, N. and Goss, S. (2000) *Evidence-Based Counselling and Psychological Therapies: Research and Applications*. London: Sage.

Sackett, D. L., Richardson, W. S., Rosenberg, W. and Haynes, R. B. (1997) *Evidence-Based Medicine: How to Practise and Teach EBM*. London: Churchill Livingstone.

Salgado, J. F. (1997) The five factor model of personality and job performance in the European community. *Journal of Applied Psychology 82*, 30–43.

Sapolsky, R. M. (1998) *Why Zebras Don't Get Ulcers: An Updated Guide to Stress, Stress-related Diseases and Coping*. Basingstoke: Macmillan.

Savickas, M. L. (1993) Career counselling in the postmodern era. *Journal of Cognitive Psychotherapy 17*, 205–15.

Scanlon, S. (1986) A matter of taste ... and type. *The Type Reporter 2*, 2–10.

Schein, E. H. (1993) *Career Anchors: Discovering Your Real Values*. London: Pfeiffer & Co rev. edn.

Schneider, B. (1987) The people make the place. *Personnel Psychology 40*, 437–53.

Schneider, B., Kristof, A. L., Goldstein, H. W. and Smith, B. W. (1997) What is this thing called fit? In N. Anderson and P. Herriot (eds) *International Handbook of Selection and Assessment*. London: Wiley.

Seligman, M. E. P. (1995) *What You Can Change ... And What You Can't*. New York: Fawcett Columbine.

Shelton, J. (1996) Health, stress and coping. In A. L. Hammer (ed.) *MBTI Applications*. Palo Alto, CA: CPP.

Smith, J. B. (1993) Teachers' grading styles: the languages of Thinking and Feeling. *Journal of Psychological Type 26*, 37–41.

Smith, T. W. and Spiro III, A. (2002) Personality, health and aging: prolegomenon for the next generation. *Journal of Research in Personality 36*, 363–94.

Smyth, J. M. (1998) Written emotional expression: effect sizes, outcome types, and moderating variables. *Journal of Consulting and Clinical Psychology 66*, 174–84.

Sparks, K., Faragher, B. and Cooper, C. L. (2001) Well-being and occupational health in the 21st century workplace. *Journal of Occupational and Organizational Psychology 74*, 489–509.

Spera, S. P., Buhrfeind, E. D. and Pennebaker, J. W. (1994) Creative writing and coping with job loss. *Academy of Management Journal 37*, 722–33.

Styron, B. (2002) The Center for Applications of Psychological Type: a history. *Journal of Psychological Type 61*, 63–6.

Taylor, P. and Small, B. (2002) Asking applicants what they would do versus what they did do: A meta-analytic comparison of situational and past behaviour employment interview questions. *Journal of Occupation and Organizational Psychology 75*, 277–94.

Taylor, P. and Small, B. (2003) Question format in the structured employment interview. *Selection and Development Review 19, 1*, 15–19.

Terkel, S. (1972) *Working*. New York: Avon.

Thayer, R. E. (1987) Energy, tiredness, and tension effects of a sugar snack versus moderate exercise. *Journal of Personality and Social Psychology 52*, 119–25.

Thayer, R. E. (1996) *The Origin of Everyday Moods: Managing Energy, Tension, and Stress*. New York: Oxford University Press.

Thomas, H. C. and Anderson, N. (2002) Selecting and developing employees for optimal Person–Organisation fit. *Selection and Development Review 18*, 3–8.

Thompson, H. L. (1996a) *Jung's Function – Attitudes Explained*. Watkinsville, GA: Worm-hole Publications.

Thompson, H. L. (1996b) 'Natural' reactions to 360° feedback. *Bulletin of Psychological Type 19*, 14–18.

Thompson, H. L. (1998) Type languages, dialects, styles and the extraverted function: is there a relationship? Unpublished paper, High Performing Systems, Inc.

Thompson, H. L. (1999) Multiple-modality feedback systems for type. *Bulletin of Psychological Type 22*, 14–18.

Tieger, P. D. and Barron-Tieger, B. (2000) *Just Your Type*. London: Little, Brown & Co.

Tieger, P. D. and Barron-Teiger, B. (2001) *Do What You Are*. London: Little, Brown & Co., 3rd edn.

Trinder, L., with Reynolds, S. (eds) (2000) *Evidence-Based Practice: A Critical Appraisal*. Oxford: Blackwell.

VanSant, S. (2003) *Wired for Conflict: The Role of Personality in Resolving Differences*. Gainesville, FL: CAPT.

Walck, C. L. (1992) The relationship between Indicator type and 'true type': slight preferences and the verification process. *The Journal of Psychological Type 23*, 17–21.

Walck, C. L. (1996) Management and leadership. In A. L. Hammer (ed.) *MBTI Applications*. Palo Alto, CA: CPP.

Wennik, R. S. (1999) *Your Personality Prescription*. New York: Kensington Books.

Wessely, S. (2001) Randomised controlled trials: the gold standard. In C. Mace, S. Moorey and B. Roberts (eds) *Evidence in the Psychological Therapies*. Hove: Brunner-Routledge.

Wimbush, E. (1994) A moderate approach to promoting physical activity: the evidence and implications. *Health Education Journal 53*, 322–6.

Woodruffe, C. (2001) Promotional intelligence. *People Management* January, 26–9.

Young, R. A. and Collin, A. (2000) Introduction: framing the future of career. In A. Collin and R. A. Young (eds) *The Future of Career*. Cambridge: Cambridge University Press.

Zimbardo, P. and Boyd, J. N. (1999) Putting time in perspective: a valid, reliable individual differences metric. *Journal of Personality and Social Psychology 77*, 1271–88.

Index